THE PEOPLE'S
PRINCESS

THE PEOPLE'S
PRINCESS

CHERISHED MEMORIES OF

Diana,

PRINCESS OF WALES,

FROM THOSE WHO KNEW HER BEST

EDITED BY

LARRY KING

CROWN PUBLISHERS NEW YORK

Copyright © 2007 by Larry King and Bill Adler Books, Inc.

All rights reserved.
Published in the United States by Crown Publishers, an imprint of the
Crown Publishing Group, a division of Random House, Inc., New York.
www.crownpublishing.com

Crown is a trademark and the Crown colophon is a registered trademark of
Random House, Inc.

Library of Congress Cataloging-in-Publication Data
    The People's princess : cherished memories of Diana, Princess of Wales,
    from those who knew her best / edited by Larry King.—1st ed.
      1. Diana, Princess of Wales, 1961–1997—Friends and associates.
    2. Diana, Princess of Wales, 1961–1997—Appreciation. 3. Princesses—
    Great Britain—Biography. I. King, Larry, 1933– II. Title.
    DA591.A45D53553 2007
    941.085092—dc22
    [B]   2007006731

ISBN 978-0-307-33953-9

Printed in the United States of America

DESIGN BY BARBARA STURMAN

Photographs by Tim Graham, copyright © by Tim Graham

10 9 8 7 6 5 4 3 2 1

First Edition

This book is dedicated in loving memory to
Diana, Princess of Wales,
on the tenth anniversary of her death.

These stories have been collected in tribute to her
undying character as we continue to mourn and
celebrate the life of such an inspiring person.
Diana, thank you for the gift of these memories.

Acknowledgments

This book would not have been possible without the dedicated editorial work of William Schrom and the staff of Bill Adler Books in New York. My sincere thanks to Steve Ross, Luke Dempsey, and Lindsey Moore at Crown Publishers, and Jeanne Welsh and the staff of Adler Robin Books in Washington, D.C. I would also like to give special regards to Bill and Gloria Adler and Katrina Milligan.

Finally, I would like to gratefully acknowledge Ingrid Seward for her invaluable assistance from the United Kingdom. Her tremendous experience and insight made this book a reality.

Contents

Foreword by Larry King 1
Introduction by Ingrid Seward 6

MEMORIES OF DIANA

Dickie Arbiter 11
Lord Jeffrey Archer 18
Jacques Azagury 21
Tyra Banks 25
Harry Benson 26
Christopher Biggins 31
Manolo Blahnik 35
Pattie Boyd 36
Sarah Bradford 40
Sir Richard Branson 43
Barbara Bush 46
Dr. Jane Collins 47
Joan Collins, OBE 49

Esteban Cortazar 54
Paul Costelloe 56
Tessa Dahl 60
Colleen Denney, PhD 71
Dharmendra 75
Nora Dunn 77
Richard, Earl of Bradford 80
Barbara Eden 83
Meredith Etherington-Smith 86
Rosie Fisher and Adam Dale 90
Daniel Galvin Sr., OBE 93
Sonia Gandhi 95
Tim Graham 97
Joan Hanger 103
Nigel Havers 109
Patrick Jephson 116
Diane Louise Jordan 122
Richard Kay 128
Larry King 133
Twiggy Lawson 136
Darren McGrady 139
Heather Mills 143
Piers Morgan 145
Bruce Oldfield, OBE 158
Robert Powell 163
Alberto Repossi 167

Zandra Rhodes 169
Sir Cliff Richard 171
Rakesh Roshan 173
David Sassoon 176
Ingrid Seward 178
Ned Sherrin 185
Simone Simmons 188
Cornelio Sommaruga 194
Taki 196
Chris Tarrant, OBE 200
Penny Thornton 204
Donald Trump 210
Catherine Walker 211
Ken Wharfe 212

DIANA: A TIME LINE

219

FOREWORD
BY LARRY KING

As an interviewer and a television personality, I have had the opportunity to talk with thousands of interesting and important people from all walks of life, including actors, politicians, royals, musicians, authors, and academics—all of whom have vastly different interpretations of countless issues. However, there have been only a few times in my career that I have experienced the level of community that occurred when Diana, Princess of Wales, died tragically ten years ago. All of these differing opinions and interpretations seemed to fade away, and the entire world grieved as one. At that point, I understood the wonder that was Diana's spirit, and I continue to see it and discuss it today. The many stories and comments within these pages powerfully show the timelessness of Diana's compassion, and we will always come back to her as an undying source of inspiration.

August 2007 will mark the tenth anniversary of Diana's untimely death, and I remember her in my own personal way, as does everybody whose story is included here. Each reader will add his or her own memory to this collection, and thus this book is, inevitably, an incomplete work; it is our collective remembrances of Diana that make up this tribute. Some of the stories here have been told before, yet most of them will be new to readers, and each moment we dwell in them revives our fundamental need for closure, to say goodbye to such a remarkable human being.

There have been many books published in the last ten years about Diana, Princess of Wales. Undoubtedly, there will be many more books published about her in the next ten, twenty, even thirty years. On one level, this is just a continuation of the media intensity she experienced throughout her life, sometimes a harsh reminder of the realities of celebrity life. More important, this attention reflects our general need to remember the lady who moved so many hearts all over the world, and how we continue to draw insight from an individual who made such a tremendous impact during her tragically short lifetime. The fact is that many of us still have strong feelings about Diana, and we need to have these feelings heard. For all of us, this need comes from a deep reservoir of love and friendship that is still as strong today as it was ten years ago.

Yes, there have been many books written about Diana. Most of these books tell specific stories from individual people, and provide many different (often conflicting) views of a remarkable woman with so many sides. However, while these books can help us understand her life, her troubles, her successes, and her interests, they oftentimes show us only one facet of a person who lived such a multifaceted life. Diana was a beautiful princess, a tireless charity worker, a good friend, a loving mother, a striking fashion icon, and, above all, an unbelievably warm spirit to all she encountered. She was, in the most concise terms, the people's princess. She was a princess for everybody, and she affected all of us in unique and powerful ways.

This book is unique in that it reflects Diana's many sides—she had many talents and passions, and all of these are touched upon in the interesting stories within these pages. Some of Diana's closest friends discuss her approachability and tremendous sense of humor—even in the face of criticism and hardship. Her colleagues in charitable causes such as land-mine awareness and

AIDS relief remember her unprecedented courage and support. We all remember the images of her holding and talking with victims of AIDS and land mines, and the pictures still serve as encouragement for the entire world to take action. As an innovative and stimulating fashion icon, Diana worked with dozens of the world's leading names in style, and many of them recount their encounters with the delightful and stunning Princess. Running throughout all of these different memories and observations is an overwhelming sense of the humanity she brought with her to every varied aspect of her life.

Although most of the people who contributed to this book were fortunate enough to meet and work with Diana at some point, many never had this opportunity and thus speak for all of us who mostly admired her from afar. This is testament to the effect she had on the world as a whole. By reaching out to us through her countless appearances on television and in magazines, she established a personal relationship with so many distant supporters. I feel that, if given the opportunity, Diana would have happily sat down with each of us and talked and listened, eager to sympathize with whatever our concerns might have been.

Diana was the people's princess, and as such she traveled relentlessly. Although a princess and a member of British royalty, she saw herself more as an international character—a woman without borders. The impressive individuals who share the following stories reflect Diana's far reach. India, Italy, Switzerland, Japan, Australia, and Morocco are just a few of the many countries that are represented here. Diana broke the barriers of nationality and saw everyone for who they were—first and foremost, human beings and extended members of her family.

—LARRY KING
August 2007

INTRODUCTION
BY INGRID SEWARD

*D*iana, Princess of Wales, was many things to many people. Headstrong and impulsive. Compassionate and practical. Happy and sad. Beautiful and glamorous and funny. She was certainly not an intellectual, but she was quick-witted with a sense of fun and an infectious giggle.

She developed from a gauche kindergarten teacher to a stylish princess beloved for her fight against adversity. She took her work seriously because it was important to her, but she had the courage never to take herself seriously, despite her insecurity.

I first met Diana when as editor of *Majesty* magazine I was reporting on one of the Prince and Princess of Wales's first foreign tours. It was ages ago, in the early eighties, and in those halcyon days of royal reporting, the press were invited to meet the people we were being paid to write about—in this case Charles and Diana. I can remember Diana turning to us and in an arch kind of way saying, "You might think you know everything about me. But I bet you don't know how many fillings I have."

Of course, none of us knew everything about Diana in those days, but it was a source of endless fascination finding out. One of the reasons we discovered so much about her was that she was far too openhearted to bottle up her feelings. If a project caught her interest or a suffering person her eye, she wanted to discuss it, right down to the frankest detail.

Above all, she had the gift for friendship. With ordinary people. With extraordinary people and with people who meant something to her. Diana was one of those people who are able to compartmentalize their lives. Sometimes these compartments overlapped, but in her mind they always remained separate, which enabled her to switch among them without allowing them to impinge on one another. She was the same with her friends. She did not care who they were as long as they needed her. She would talk to them about their cares their hopes, their interests, and their loves. She wanted to know every detail of their lives. She knew what it was like to feel real pain and real unhappiness—that was a big part of her allure. But she liked to keep them separate.

Maybe that is why some of the people—her friends, her acquaintances, and her admirers—whose stories appear on the following pages have such diverse views. I enjoyed talking to many of them myself and helping Larry compile this unique memento of Diana ten years after her tragic death.

—INGRID SEWARD
August 2007

Memories
OF DIANA

DICKIE ARBITER

Former press secretary to Queen Elizabeth II Dickie Arbiter is a British broadcaster and journalist. He has covered royalty, heads of state, and other international personalities for more than thirty years, and his unique access to so many important figures of recent history makes him one of the most experienced commentators in Britain. He is currently in high demand throughout the world as a lecturer and commentator on radio and television.

I met Diana, Princess of Wales, at Buckingham Palace a couple of days before she became the "new royal kid on the block" at her wedding, which took place on Wednesday, July 29, 1981. The event stopped the world for most of the day, as a global television audience of 750 million, more than half a million spectators lining the wedding route from Buckingham Palace, and twenty-five hundred guests in St. Paul's Cathedral witnessed "shy Di" say "I will" to her Prince Charming and prepared to "ride off into the sunset to live happily ever after." As one of the commentators on that memorable day, I, too, was carried along by the euphoria of the royal match.

My first impression of Diana on that Monday morning was one of a nervous, apprehensive girl, barely out of her teens, hiding smiling eyes behind her fringe. I wondered how she was going to cope on her big day, whether she could pull off the pomp and ceremony, and how she was going to handle being a newly paid-up member of the Royal Firm. In fact, she did carry the day off, much to her credit, and mercifully she was unaware of what lay ahead of her.

When I joined Buckingham Palace, I'd spent more than twenty years in radio and television, eight of them accredited to the palace as a royal reporter. That naive twenty-year-old girl I met on a sunny July morning was very different from the twenty-six-year-old woman I went to work for six years later.

So when, as poacher turned gamekeeper, I walked through the palace gates, I knew the job wasn't going to be easy, but I was reasonably prepared for the royal ride ahead. My new job included being part of the team responsible for the Queen, as well as advising and managing media relations for the Prince and Princess of Wales, both as a duo and as individuals whenever they went solo.

Cracks were already beginning to form in the "golden couple's" marriage, and as every day brought endless media inquiries about who was doing what, where, with whom, and why, it became increasingly difficult to paper over them.

Charles and Diana crisscrossed the United Kingdom and the globe for eleven years and developed a reputation for being the best double act in the business. They made a lot of people happy in the process. However, during their later tours, questions about where they were going and why became less important for the watching media than how they were coping with the "ordeal" of being in each other's company. The media were always slightly ahead of the game with their questions, but confronting the royals was never going to provide the answers.

During her years on the royal road, Diana did wonderful work. With one simple gesture to HIV patients and leprosy victims, she exploded the "do-not-touch" myth. She drew attention to the plight of the homeless, drug addicts, land-mine victims, and other victims of ill fortune. She was also a very good full-time mother, but, sadly, she became a part-time wife.

I traveled a great deal with her at home and abroad, and we spent many hours in each other's company. We occasionally swam together early in the morning or late at night, and we had many laughs—she had a great sense of humor. She was intoxicating, and any man she met immediately fell in love with her—including me.

But we also had our differences of opinion. She was very good with people she met in her public life but not always so good with the people who worked for her, some of whom she treated appallingly. She blew hot and cold—you were either in or out; there was no halfway house—and there were periods when we did not speak to each other. She would freeze you out, something she was prone to do to anyone who got too close to her.

Since her sudden, violent, and shocking death in August 1997, many people have crawled out of the woodwork, contributing to newspaper and magazine articles or publishing books, all of them claiming to be friends. In reality, Diana had so few real friends that you could count them on one hand. The rest of these self-proclaimed friends were swept up in Diana's wake and were, at best, acquaintances, basking in her reflected glory. Some were just straphangers, hoping one day to cash in, as so many have done since that fateful night in Paris ten years ago.

I stopped working for Diana after her separation from the Prince, but since I lived in the environs of Kensington Palace, we were able to keep in touch.

What struck me most about her was that despite the acrimony that engulfed both her and the Prince following their separation in 1992, she never lost her sense of humor. Her infamous television interview is largely remembered for her wry comment, "There were three of us in this marriage, so it was a bit crowded." Once I came across her rummaging in the trunk of a new car. "Not a German car for an English princess, surely," I said. Quick as a flash she replied, "Well, at least it's more reliable than a German husband."

She was also incredibly generous and loved giving presents, always wanting you to open them in front of her. She always sent a card for my birthday, and when I turned fifty, she hosted a lunch for me at Kensington Palace for twenty of my family and friends.

Diana wasn't beautiful, but she did have the looks, charisma, and glamour that turned heads. She'd been on the front page of every newspaper and magazine worldwide, and hardly a day went by that a photograph of her wasn't published somewhere. She wasn't an intellectual, but she more than made up for that by being very smart and streetwise.

I won't ever forget the day Diana died or the days that followed. So much history was written in those six days between her death and when she was laid to rest at the Spencer family's ancestral home at Althorp.

I was alongside the Queen when she joined mourners outside the Buckingham Palace gates to see for herself the vast bank of flowers that had built up over the week. I was concerned about the reception that she and the Duke of Edinburgh might receive, given the vehemently critical press commentary during the week. I needn't have worried; as the Queen walked through the palace gates, the subdued crowd applauded in sympathy and offered words of comfort.

In this incident, as in so many aspects of Diana's life, the media headlines told only part of the story. She once claimed she was "hunted and haunted" by the media and even went so far as to describe herself as "a media toy." At times she was to blame for this, courting them for her own agenda. Having traveled alongside her on her journey from that fairy-tale wedding to her lying at rest in St. James's Palace's Chapel Royal, I was determined to play my part in ensuring that the media gave her a farewell that befitted not just her status but her impact as an individual who sought always to contribute positively to public life even while she wrestled with her private troubles.

Since her death, the same media have speculated on the advent of a "new Diana" when Princes William and Harry eventually marry and bring their wives into the Royal Firm. But their mother was a one-off. I don't want a new Diana; I was happy with the one we had. She did wonderful work for charity and made many ordinary people happy, and for that we should be grateful. I missed her when she died so tragically in a Paris underpass, I still miss her ten years on, and I will probably always miss her.

LORD JEFFREY ARCHER

❧

Lord Jeffrey Archer is an accomplished British author and former member of Parliament and deputy chairman of the Conservative Party. His novel *Kane and Abel* reached number one on the *New York Times* bestseller list and was eventually made into a miniseries. He was a good friend of Diana's and helped her fund-raise for numerous charities.

I first met Princess Diana at a Red Cross function twenty-five years ago, when I was the charity auctioneer and she was the guest of honor. After that, she regularly requested that I carry out the same duties at all her charity functions, which, of course, I was delighted to do. Over the years, what had started as a professional relationship developed into a personal friendship, and we often dined privately in each other's homes.

In 1993, the prime minister (John Major) asked me to be with her on the day the palace and the government were announcing that she would be retiring from public life. I think my saddest memory of that occasion was taking her home to Kensington Palace after she had received a standing ovation from the thousand people who had listened to her speech at the Hilton Hotel. I later learned from her butler that she had a TV dinner and sat alone in the drawing room before going to bed.

I learned of the Princess's tragic death when Sir Nicholas Lloyd, the newspaper editor, phoned me at four o'clock in the morning on August 31. I refused to turn on the television or the radio, as I attempted to convince myself that it couldn't be true.

Her funeral at Westminster Abbey was one of the most poignant events I have ever attended, and I was touched by Earl Spencer's kindness in seating Mary and me with the family in the private part of the abbey.

Following the hugely successful sale of her dresses in June 1997, at her request I purchased the remaining four hundred catalogs for £27,000, and the Princess promised to sign them for any auction she attended, where, on average, ten years ago, they would make £5,000 each. But sadly, her premature death meant that we didn't make the million pounds for the Red Cross that she hoped to achieve for the remaining unsigned copies. Ironically, I still have a few left, which I continue to auction, as long as the person sends the check to the British Red Cross.

I'm reminded of her almost daily, because whenever I do an auction, I always realize how much more I would raise if she was sitting there. She was an amazing servant who, in her seventeen years of public life, made a genuine difference in many people's lives.

I am fortunate to have the most beautiful signed, silver-framed photograph, a magnificent pair of cuff links, and several private letters, should I ever forget the minor role I played in her amazing life.

Diana would have been surprised by the public's unbelievable response to her death, and even more surprised that ten years later this interest has not waned. But then they don't make them like that very often, do they.

JACQUES AZAGURY

Moroccan-born couturier Jacques Azagury trained at St. Martin's School of Art in London. In his final-year show, he was hailed as one of the most promising new designers and launched straight into his first collection. He opened his flagship store in Knightsbridge, London, in 1987.

I was introduced to the Princess by Anna Harvey from *Vogue* in the mid-eighties when she was still experimenting with clothes and far from the fashion icon she later became. As soon as I saw how stunning she was, I urged her to make more of her allure, but she resisted, because she was afraid of drawing criticism from the Royal Family. Her natural instinct was to hide away her beauty, and it took years before she was able to believe she was actually a beautiful woman.

After the pain of her divorce from Prince Charles had subsided, she grew in confidence, and the Diana I saw was no longer the insecure, uncertain woman who would come into the salon with her shoulders stooped and head bowed. She looked her very best—slim but not thin, fit and glowing with joy, standing tall with her head held high.

She prided herself on being normal and didn't stand on ceremony. She made everyone comfortable when she came into the shop, sometimes unannounced, and if I was with another client, she would say, "Carry on. I'll wait." Whenever I visited her at Kensington Palace, she would bound to the door and greet me herself, rather than have the butler show me into the drawing room. She didn't like formality; she found it oppressive.

As well as looking gorgeous, she loved wearing clothes and dressing up. She knew people expected it of her, and she did not like to disappoint anyone. I made clothes for her for almost ten years, but our heyday together was in the mid- to late nineties, when she was free to be herself and was not afraid of wearing clothes that made her look sexy, but not like a sex symbol. One of her favorites was a beaded, full-length, backless dress, which she wore to a political dinner in 1994. She was conscious that the occasion was quite serious, so we used understated colors—graphite on black. But the thigh-high split gave the dress a sexy twist. It became famous when she wore it for her first photo session with Patrick Demarchelier, with her hair slicked back.

The Princess was dedicated to her campaign for a ban on land mines. After she had returned from Angola in 1997, she came into the salon, and when she was telling me about her trip, she was almost crying. She explained how terrible things were there, and that she was trying to make people aware of it. It was so important to her that she agonized over what to wear for the charity dinner in New York on behalf of the Red Cross. She wanted it to be just right so that people would concentrate on what she had to say, not what she was wearing. Eventually, she chose a dazzling long red dress—red in honor of the Red Cross—with a high neckline. I wanted her to turn heads when she was dancing, so I persuaded her to allow me to put a deep V shape at the back, which was perfect.

The last dress she ordered from me was in late June 1997, when she was looking for a "statement frock" for a charity dinner at the Tate Gallery to be held on July 1—her thirty-sixth birthday. I could see that she finally felt free, unburdened, as if everything that had frightened or troubled her had all come into focus. She saw it all for what it was and was no longer afraid. It is difficult to explain how extraordinary she was. There was an unmistakable determination about her, none of her usual uncertainty. She was no longer suffering, that's the only way I can describe it.

I visited her at Kensington Palace for the final fitting on the day before her birthday, and she was mischievous and full of fun. She had just been photographed by Mario Testino and was thrilled that he had taught her to walk like a runway model. She couldn't wait to demonstrate and paraded up and down, catwalk-style, shimmying and showing she had learned to "work the train"—to walk and turn without the train of the dress getting in the way. We were both giggling our heads off, and she was enjoying herself like a child.

It was the last time I ever saw her.

TYRA BANKS

More recently known for her role as host and judge on CW's hit reality television show *America's Next Top Model*, Tyra Banks is widely considered to be one of the most famous and successful supermodels in the world. She is also an author, actress, musician, and noted talk-show host.

I remember like it was yesterday. August 31, 1997, the day it was first announced that Diana had been in a car crash. The media stated that she had been rushed to a hospital and doctors were working to revive her. I sat alone on the edge of my bed, glued to the television, and hoped and prayed that the outcome would be positive. When the news of her death came, I cried nonstop for three hours. I just could not understand why. Why now? Why her? Why so tragically?

The most amazing thing about Diana was that although she was a princess, the struggles she went through were those of the everyday woman. She had been royalty, but she was just like all of us. Someone to aspire to, yet someone to relate to. And when she left the earth, she left a void that can never be filled.

HARRY BENSON

Scottish-born Harry Benson is an internationally renowned portrait and war photographer whose work has been featured in many prestigious magazines, including *Life, Vanity Fair, People,* and *The New Yorker.* He has photographed many icons of the twentieth century, including the Beatles, Michael Jackson, Elizabeth Taylor, and, of course, Diana.

I was to photograph the Princess in Covent Garden going into some opening— the ballet, the opera, I forget which. It was November, and it was bleak and cold. I had to be there hours ahead of time to get a good position. At 7:30 p.m. Diana stepped out of her limousine. I had never seen her looking better. Smiling, waving. Cheers went up all around. She walked up the line of photographers and gave me a beautiful smile, and my camera didn't work. A photographer's worst nightmare. She walked on about four yards, saw what happened, walked back, and stood there until I got the photo. It sold around the world. Now you ask me why the press loved her. That's why.

We (the photographers) also loved her because the public craved reading about her and seeing her photograph. Her picture would sell newspapers and magazines like no other.

Diana was always able to come up with something to get the world's attention, and every London paper had a "Diana watcher" assigned to chart her every move. Sometimes Diana would call a photographer she liked and tell him where she would be; she understood the business and knew that good pictures of her were going to enhance her image—the image she presented and the world fell in love with.

I myself am a photojournalist, born in Glasgow and based in America. On the occasions that I photographed the Princess, she was always aware of her surroundings. She was beautiful, smiling, and considerate; there was always excitement around her every move. People believed that she actually cared about them, and that was why they responded so openly with their love.

When Diana was to be in Glasgow in 1992, I was given an assignment to photograph her visit. On the route she would be taking, I saw a little girl holding flowers who had been lifted over the barrier to wait for Diana.

As she always responded warmly to children, I positioned myself there and waited, making a calculated guess that Diana would stop. She walked up to the little girl, bent down, smiling and talking to the child all the while, and accepted the flowers—and I got the photo. Most other royals would have just glanced down, waved, and then would have been on their way, their work over.

She was the fairy-tale princess in a fairy-tale marriage, and when that myth was exposed, she was perceived as the hard-done-by wife of a husband who, on their wedding day, wore cuff links given to him by his mistress. Diana was forgiven her transgressions and idolized even more. Public sympathy was with her. And in death, she became the most revered icon of the twentieth or any other century.

Diana didn't pose only for the "social" photographers. She had a very good rapport with most of the photographers who covered her every day. And their photos influenced the world. Even when she went to the South of France with Dodi Al Fayed, she apparently called two photographers she knew to tell them where she would be. And then there was Paris. You've got to understand, the photographers weren't hanging around the Ritz Hotel on a Saturday night because they wanted to. It was because every magazine and newspaper around the world wanted pictures of the mother of the future king of England with her new boyfriend.

The paparazzi were blamed for her death. Only President Clinton did not jump to that conclusion, asking everyone when he made his statement to wait to find out what had caused the crash. And the cause was drunk driving. Princess Diana should be the poster child for Mothers Against Drunk Driving.

I was in London the day of her funeral. Never in history was there such an outpouring of grief from around the world. London was a sea of flowers, the likes of which had never been seen before. I followed the casket down the Mall as it passed the mourners. There were gasps and cries and shrieks of "Oh, Diana." Grown men were weeping and shaking alongside their devastated wives and children. Only when I saw the flowers and the mourners did I realize to what extent this woman had touched the lives of so many around the world.

Everything was not perfect on the day of her funeral. In my opinion, we could have done without the arrogant eulogy given by her brother and the recycled song sung by Elton John, which would have been more at home in a rock concert, but otherwise it was an unforgettable day.

I don't think people so much wanted to be her as to idolize her and their idea of what she represented—a commoner who became a princess, who then became the princess of the people. I'm glad she lived during my lifetime. The phenomenon of what her life became— I don't think we'll ever see the likes of it again.

CHRISTOPHER BIGGINS

A successful and prolific British television and theater actor, Christopher Biggins is known for his lead roles in a number of acclaimed BBC original programs. Recognized for his distinctive voice and versatile style, Christopher Biggins has appeared as Nero in Robert Graves's *I, Claudius*, in *The Rocky Horror Picture Show*, and in many esteemed comedies, including *Porridge*.

The first time I met Diana was in the Savoy Hotel in London. I was in charge of an auction for a charity that she supported. She was a massive star, and although I had seen endless photographs of her, I was not prepared for the full impact of her real-life glamour. Her height, her honey-colored skin, and her blue eyes, along with her being perfectly coiffed, manicured, and dressed, made her pure Hollywood. But that was where it stopped. She had no airs and graces, no grandeur. She was simply incredibly charming and friendly, and in a few minutes I felt as if I had known her for ages. She was brilliant at putting people at ease, and part of that gift was to be totally approachable. An off-the-cuff remark, a joke here and there, a comment about her life—that did the trick.

We shared a few jokes, as much as you can in royal circles. It was an official engagement for her, and she had a lady-in-waiting and a couple of police protection officers, as well as the charity chiefs, hanging on her every word.

As I am renowned for having one of the clearest, loudest voices in the business, I get asked to do a lot of charity auctions. I enjoy working for charity, as I feel I am giving something back to the world, and on the charity trail I met the Princess again and again. I wouldn't say we became close friends, but we were always pleased to see each other. I guess I made her laugh, and I was flattered that she appeared to enjoy my company. We started a correspondence—Diana was a prolific and articulate letter writer; since she spent a lot of time on her own, she liked communicating this way. I wrote to her after she had been in Angola on her mission to ban land mines in early 1997, as I was so proud of her. She replied:

> *Dear Christopher,*
>
> I was <u>touched</u> that you took the trouble to write, having seen the documentary film of my visit to Angola. I hope the world now has a better knowledge of the suffering caused by anti personnel mines

and there will be an opportunity for me to visit some of the sixty-five other countries affected in the same manner! Your letter meant a great deal to me and I would like to send you my heartfelt thanks!

When Liza Minnelli came to town, we would always meet. On one occasion, when Liza had a new show at the Albert Hall, she rang me and asked me if I would mind looking after a friend of hers. I went backstage half an hour before the beginning of the show to pick up Liza's mystery friend, and a couple of minutes later Diana burst into Liza's dressing room, announcing that she was to be my date.

We had just sat down in the front row when Liza's sidekicks—ten women—came onto the stage and started an act with the lights full on. I was chatting to Diana about a photograph I had seen of her embracing her boys, and she turned to me and said, "You have no idea how much they mean to me." Then the lights went down and Liza launched into her first number, which was interrupted by the women again.

It was all part of the show, but Diana didn't realize this and put her face in her hands. She looked at me through her fingers and mouthed, "How embarrassing!" Eventually, she relaxed and enjoyed Liza's magnificent performance. The sad thing was that at the end of the show, Liza and I went out to dinner, while Diana made her lonely way back to Kensington Palace to have her supper on a tray in front of the TV, as she often did. There is something very poignant about the image of her dining alone after having been the center of so much adoration and attention.

The biggest mistake of her life was falling in love with her husband. If she hadn't cared for him so much, it would have made everything easier to deal with. I don't think anyone had ever taken her aside and explained that her husband had a mistress. She was too young and too innocent and had all these ideas about living happily ever after.

Diana put the monarchy on the map. The Queen failed to realize how big Diana was and underestimated her impact on the world. She was a royal of today. She changed things, and the boys will, too. I still miss her.

MANOLO BLAHNIK

Spanish-born Manolo Blahnik is one of the most celebrated and distinguished shoe designers in the world. His women's shoes are highly coveted by the international fashion elite, and have been widely featured in popular culture, most notably on HBO's *Sex and the City*.

She was beautiful in every sense, inside as much as out, and had an aura that made her unique.

It was a privilege for me to have seen her working with charities, and the way she addressed the people she cared for will stay with me forever.

I feel honored to have served her in her lifetime.

PATTIE BOYD

Pattie Boyd, whose autobiography will be published in 2007, is the former wife of the late George Harrison and subsequently Eric Clapton. She was the inspiration for Harrison's hit song "Something" and Clapton's "Layla" and "Wonderful Tonight."

It was during my marriage to Eric that I first met Diana, Princess of Wales. We were at a lineup after a concert for the Prince's Trust—one of Prince Charles's main charities, which helps underprivileged youngsters—when the newly married couple came to shake hands with all the rockers and their wives. Charles was on the left of the group and Diana on the right. Suddenly, as if by magic, they switched sides. It was all so professional and yet she was so young. I had my hair in a chignon, and I was wearing some jewelry that Eric had designed for me, and felt quite chic, but as soon as I saw her I felt very much the rock-star wife while she was the glamorous princess.

Naturally, Diana knew who Eric was, but she turned to me and started talking to me about fame. "Clearly, you have lots of experience with the press and know how careful you have to be, and isn't it hard?" she said, with a twinkle in her eye. I was quite taken aback, as I didn't realize she knew who I was, but she obviously had been well briefed. I felt quite relaxed talking to her, and she seemed to know we had similar experiences dealing with the problems of being married to famous men. I think it was sometime in 1981, so she had only been married a few months and was not quite the iconic figure she later became. She was very beautiful even then. I think it was her perfect skin and bright-blue eyes that struck me most.

I met her again later at an event for the charity Birthright, which I supported when she was its patron. This time I found her more guarded and even more beautiful, but the lightness she had when I first met her had disappeared. I knew she had by then realized what a responsibility she had taken on becoming a royal princess and being photographed and stared at, whatever she did. I could relate to that.

When I married George Harrison in 1966, I didn't realize what it was like to be with someone who was so famous. I was the model who married a Beatle. Diana was the nursery-school teacher who married a prince. Although our husbands were from totally different backgrounds—George was a working-class boy from Liverpool, while Charles was a Prince of the Realm—each had his own cross to bear.

When you marry someone like that, you not only marry him but also his life, and you don't think about the consequences until afterward. This is what happened to Diana, and this is what happened to me.

Like her, I became vulnerable and insecure. There were so many girls more beautiful than me who wanted to be with my husband. I was nineteen when I met George, and I married him soon after, as Diana did with Charles. But unlike her, I felt joyously happy. I wanted all my girlfriends to join in my happiness, and I wanted my husband to meet them all and love them as much as I did. George did indeed meet and like all my family and friends.

Without that, I couldn't have coped with all the pressures that come with fame. It wasn't my fame, but I was surrounded with it and lived in its world. Diana had none of this support, and I am convinced that it would have helped her so much if she had. Instead, Prince Charles loathed her friends and certainly had little interest in her family. She was isolated and surrounded by people who paid homage to her husband, not her.

One day, I said to George, "I just find it so worrying that you find it necessary to surround yourself with all these yes-men."

"I would hate to be surrounded by 'no' men," he replied.

I guess that sums the whole unreal world that both Diana and I lived through. I escaped and she didn't.

SARAH BRADFORD

৵৵

Sarah Bradford's *Diana* is published by Viking Penguin. Her other biographies include *Disraeli,* named Book of the Year by the *New York Times; Princess Grace,* written with the cooperation of Prince Rainier and the Kelly family; *George VI* (published in the United States as *The Reluctant King*), which George's daughter, the Queen, is said to keep on her desk; *Splendours and Miseries: The Life of Sacheverell Sitwell,* written at the request of Sitwell's family, who made the archives available to her for the first time; and two international bestsellers, *Elizabeth: A Biography of Her Majesty the Queen* and *America's Queen: The Life of Jacqueline Kennedy Onassis.*

I was out of the country when Diana died, returning to London in time to commentate on her funeral for a U.S. network. Sitting in a darkened studio lit only by the extraordinary images transmitted by the television, I found it hard to grasp or even believe what was happening. All this pomp, all this grief—it might have been the funeral of a U.S. president (JFK immediately springs to mind) or a figure of the stature of Winston Churchill. Yet what was being celebrated here was the life and tragic death of a thirty-six-year-old English girl who had become known to, even worshipped by, millions of people worldwide. Why, and how, this had come about were the questions that struck all of us at the time: the answers to which I sought over the following years as I worked on her biography, piecing together the story of her life, interviewing people who had known or worked for her, or even just encountered her.

From her childhood, Diana had had the feeling that she was destined for something special, that she would *be* somebody. There never was a chance that she would have, as people have surmised, settled down and led the life of a country gentleman's wife, walking the dogs and rearing a handful of children. Her sense of destiny was far too strong. When she was a child, her stepfather, Peter Shand Kydd, nicknamed her "Duch," short for "Duchess," for her imperious ways. Although she did not know it, she carried the genes of the strong, willful, often difficult women among her Spencer ancestors: Georgiana, Duchess of Devonshire, and Sarah, Duchess of Marlborough. And she had that ability to connect with the camera, which is an outstanding feature of all modern icons. Together with that innate sense of destiny, it was a quality she shared with two of my previous subjects: Grace Kelly (who also married a prince and died as a result of a car crash) and Jacqueline Kennedy Onassis.

Ten years after Diana's death, she still arouses strong passions; there are pro- and anti-Diana factions. To the antis, she was a stupid but at the same time manipulative woman whose importance was exaggerated and whose disappearance was a good thing for the British monarchy. For her partisans, she was a misunderstood and mistreated saint, sacrificed on the altar of the hereditary succession to the British throne. There is truth on both sides: Diana was tough and gutsy; she fought back with methods that were not always pretty, manipulating the press in her battle against her husband, bringing her fame into the equation in her fight against establishment attempts to extinguish her. She made huge mistakes, among which the *Panorama* interview was a fatal one, ensuring her final expulsion from the charmed circle of the family she had married into. But she had a quality of empathy that made her truly extraordinary, and an ability to reach out to the poor and the sick of whatever nationality that ranked her with the popular medieval saints. Seasoned journalists like William Deedes, who accompanied her on every step of her anti-land-mine campaign in Angola, could see that her tireless compassion was genuine.

SIR RICHARD BRANSON

Sir Richard Branson is the founder and chairman of the
Virgin Group of companies. An immensely successful
entrepreneur, philanthropist, and television star, Sir Richard was knighted by Queen Elizabeth II in 1999. In 2002,
Sir Richard was voted one of the "100 Greatest Britons"
in a poll sponsored by the BBC.

I was fortunate enough to know Diana for
most of her adult life. For most of those
years, I saw the sunny side of her personality. She was
great fun, she was very caring, she did much for charity, and yet she was no saint and certainly wouldn't
have wished to be portrayed as one. On her death, the
outpouring of grief was understandable, but she would
have smiled wryly if she had seen the deference paid to
her in the weeks following it.

Of course, Diana knew the importance of the publicity she generated for charity—who will ever forget
those incredible photographs of a lonely figure in the
midst of a land-mine field—but I don't believe she was
ever truly aware of how many people in the world
loved her. Diana may not have known, but through
their grief, I'm sure Harry and William could not have

failed to be moved by the public display of emotion over the loss of their mother. Millions of arms across the world were hugging them close.

And a mother she certainly was—with William and Harry, Diana would holiday on our island, Necker, in the British Virgin Islands. She loved it there because by and large she could pull up the drawbridge and frolic with her kids away from of the eyes of the photographers.

She was a very loyal friend. When British Airways tried to drive Virgin out of business, I took them to court and won a celebrated victory. Lord King, BA's chairman, stepped down, and later a handwritten note from Diana was delivered to me. It was just three words: "Hurray! Love, Diana."

She also named one of our planes *Lady in Red*. We took a flight in *Lady in Red* with Diana commentating from the cockpit with William on her lap. As we flew past Windsor Castle, her voice came over the loud-speaker: "On our right, you have Grandma's house!" Everyone on the plane fell about laughing.

Eighteen years later, my daughter Holly was enjoying Prince William's twenty-first birthday party at "Grandma's house." A giant elephant had been constructed out of ice, and "shots" were being poured down its trunk and young ladies were drinking from it.

Holly found herself kneeling with her mouth around it, glancing upward to see the Queen looking down at her disapprovingly.

If Diana had still been alive, she would have laughed until she cried.

BARBARA BUSH

Wife of the forty-first president of the United States, George H. W. Bush, and mother of the current president, George W. Bush, Barbara Bush was First Lady from 1989 to 1993. As First Lady, she focused on such important issues as literacy, homelessness, and AIDS awareness.

My most memorable times spent with the lovely Princess Diana were visiting hospitals in the USA and England. She had an extraordinary ability to talk to the sick and dying—to put them at ease and to bring hope and joy to their lives. This was a special gift, and she gave it graciously.

DR. JANE COLLINS

As chief executive of the Great Ormond Street Hospital (GOSH) for Children NHS Trust, Dr. Jane Collins oversees the hospital of which Diana was president during her charitable career. GOSH specializes in the treatment and research of childhood illness and remains one of the most notable facilities in this field in the world.

I am delighted on behalf of Great Ormond Street Hospital for Children and personally to write about Princess Diana, who was a great friend to this hospital, of which she was president.

Before becoming chief executive, I was a consultant neurologist at GOSH, and on one of her many visits I was lucky enough to take Princess Diana to meet some of my patients on the ward. I was slightly overwhelmed by her presence when we met, and although Princess Diana was very friendly, I thought she was almost a little shy with me. But the minute she arrived on the ward and was with the children and their families, she became totally relaxed, sitting on the sides of the beds and treating each child she met and his or her parents as if they were the only people in the world she wanted to talk to.

Princess Diana was a frequent visitor to the hospital, and many of our staff have told me of their similar experience when she visited their wards. I'm sure we all remember the day she died as if it was yesterday and will never forget our sense of grief and personal loss. But our abiding memory is of a warm, compassionate princess, with a deep affection for babies and children, comfortable with people from every background, of whatever nationality, and in whatever circumstances they met.

JOAN COLLINS, OBE

Joan Collins is first and foremost an actress, but she is also a bestselling author, an accomplished producer, a successful entrepreneur, and a devoted mother. Joan is internationally renowned for her role as Alexis Carrington in the TV drama *Dynasty*. Published in 2006, her latest book, *The Art of Living Well,* is an inspirational self-help book. Joan is touring in a play called *Legends* with Linda Evans from *Dynasty*. They opened in Toronto and will be touring the States, ending up in New York.

first met Diana, Princess of Wales, in the early eighties at a charity gala in Palm Beach hosted by business tycoon Armand Hammer. When I was presented to her in the lineup, my impression was of someone very beautiful and very shy. We were surrounded by a bank of photographers shooting away madly, and she looked at me for reassurance and said, "How do you stand it?" I told her that she would get used to it, but she seemed unsure of this and told me she didn't think she ever would, as they never stopped taking pictures of her. I remember that night very well—Prince Charles asked me to dance. He was very charming and an excellent dancer.

I met Diana again several times after that, and in 1992 she came to see me in *Private Lives,* which was playing at London's Cambridge Theatre. She was very enthusiastic about the show and made a couple of jokes about the press; by that time, she confessed she was getting more used to the media attention.

The next time I had a chance to talk to her properly was at a charity dinner at Cliveden in the early nineties. She must have been married for ten years by then, and she was a different person. She was confident, witty, and sophisticated, but still full of charm. We were seated at a table of twelve and I was opposite Diana, so we could talk easily. I was wearing a sleeveless, strapless dress and it was freezing, so I asked a waiter if he would mind bringing me my fur so I could keep warm. He duly brought it to me. Unfortunately, it was a white mink, but that is what we did in the nineties.

I put the mink round my shoulders, and as I did so I looked across the table at Diana, who wagged her finger disapprovingly.

"Naughty, naughty," she said. "You mustn't wear fur—mustn't wear fur!"

Everybody at the table looked at us and laughed. I was slightly taken aback, but not wishing to appear rude and upset the guest of honor, I asked for the coat to be taken away again. I sat through the rest of the dinner freezing to death. It was a very amusing evening and Diana was in top form, but I felt myself getting colder and colder.

Two days later, I woke up with the worst case of flu I have ever had. I had a temperature of 104 degrees and remember looking up at my son, Sacha, and my brother Bill, who were standing at the foot of my bed and saying to myself, "My God, have I died because Princess Diana wouldn't let me wear my fur?"

After that, I saw her at various other places, but those are the three times I recall well. I knew all was not well with her life and I did relate to some of the problems she had, but I never realized they would become as severe as they did. She was always being followed by photographers, but in the early eighties and even in the nineties, when I was making *Dynasty*—which was incredibly popular—the paparazzi were nothing like they became later. I did not have to have bodyguards, and although people would call out to me in the street or come up to me for an autograph, it was a much safer time.

I was very sympathetic toward Diana and hoped she would find happiness. I knew Dodi Al Fayed quite well; in fact, we flew back from Los Angeles together in June the year they were killed. I asked him what he was doing, and he told me he was going to London to get a movie ready and then traveling on to Saint-Tropez, where I also have a house. I told him I hoped to see him there, but of course I never saw him again.

When they were killed, I was devastated and cried all day. I was in my house in Saint-Tropez when my assistant called me from London at 6:30 or 7:00 in the morning to tell me the news because he knew how much I admired Diana. I rushed upstairs to my girlfriend's room to tell her and we sat and watched Sky News all day, sobbing. We couldn't believe it. We were devastated, really devastated.

I called Elton John after his wonderful tribute (he sang "Candle in the Wind" at the funeral) to say "that was the greatest; she would have been so thrilled."

When we were making *Dynasty* in the early eighties I used to tear photographs of Diana out of magazines and give them to Nolan Miller (the designer) and explain that Diana's look was exactly what Alexis needed in this scene or that scene. Lots of Cossack hats and coats with frogging.

Historically, I think Diana will be remembered with a dichotomy of thoughts, as it always amazes me that so many people didn't like her. Rather like Marie Antoinette, the doomed queen of France. But there are a lot of people that admired her tremendously. I certainly did.

ESTEBAN CORTAZAR

Internationally recognized fashion prodigy Esteban Cortazar has been designing innovative clothing since his early
teens, making his unofficial debut at age fifteen at Miami
International Fashion Week in 1999. Esteban Cortazar's
garments have been featured in many respected magazines, including *W* and British *Vogue*. His collection of
ready-to-wear is in high demand and available at many
prominent stores.

*W*hen I was a young kid, the image of Princess Diana was always vivid in my mind,
since her face was on the covers of the magazines that
my mother had. Because I was so young, I didn't really
know her story or who she was except for that she was
a beautiful woman. In 1996, at the age of twelve, I
moved to Miami Beach, to live with my father above
the News Café. I quickly became interested in fashion
and surrounded myself with people in the fashion community, befriending stylish and artistic personalities,
among them Gianni Versace, who had breakfast every
morning at the News Café while I waited for my bus
to take me to school. As I began investigating his work,
I came across images of Diana dressed in Versace, and it

was then that I understood how much of a style icon she was, full of authentic elegance and effortless class. I remember seeing the beautiful photos taken of her by Mario Testino and feeling so inspired by her fresh beauty, incredible smile, and poise. When I look at those images now, I see how much he really captured her peaceful spirit and genuine soul.

In July 1997, I can remember so well seeing pictures of Diana sitting next to Sir Elton John at Gianni's funeral, and feeling the sadness in her eyes of losing a friend who had viewed her as such an inspiration and beloved muse. It was then that I decided to make an enormous collage in honor of Gianni from the images I had saved of his work, but for some reason I saved the ones of Diana in his dresses—never imagining, of course, that less than two months later we would be losing her as well. I understood why I had saved those pictures of her. I made another collage with all the images that captured her spirit and sent it to her memorial as a tribute to her and in remembrance. The collage celebrated her tenderness, her compassion toward living beings, and her being one of the greatest style icons ever to exist.

PAUL COSTELLOE

One of the most established and experienced names in British fashion, Irish-born Paul Costelloe has maintained a highly successful design label for more than twenty-five years. He was educated in Paris and Milan, and has since become known for his expertise in fabrics, primarily crisp linen and tweed.

I suppose one of my more memorable moments was when I first met Diana. First, however, there are a couple of things I will just go over very briefly. I'm Irish born with an American mother and an Irish father. I was commuting to London from Ireland at the time when I got a call to come to Kensington Palace. I got a minicab and threw some garments in the back of the car, and the driver drove me to Kensington Palace. The police at the gate were surprised to see a battered minicab—it was no black cab, if you know the difference between a black cab and a minicab in London (a minicab is half the price of a black cab and always more battered). Anyway, they asked me who I was.

I said, "I have an appointment to see Diana," and they told me to wait. They were reluctant to let me through the gates—it was during the major troubles in Northern Ireland, during the mid to late seventies and early eighties, when Belfast was blazing—but I was soon met at the door. I remember hauling my garments up the stairs of the palace. I fell. Diana came halfway down the stairs and gave me a hand with the garments. Then we went into the living room and had a lovely cup of tea, and I met the children, William and Harry. She tried on some of the garments right there in front of me. I (being a confirmed heterosexual) found her very attractive. I came back down the stairs, and half an hour later she made her selection. She was a perfect size 10 (that would be a U.S. size 8), except she was tall, so a few things had to be lengthened. She was an absolute delight. Afterward, I went into Hyde Park for the afternoon and sat on a bench. I just couldn't believe what had just happened!

That was at the peak of her career, when everything was still going fine for her. Her marriage had not yet broken up—it was a very special time. I had quite a few visits like that; Diana was always very courteous and enjoyable. She would ask the taxi driver to come in, and he would sit in the kitchen and get his tea and biscuits. This is, of course, quite uncommon, as you might imagine, even for any major home, particularly in London. She really did not have any class discrimination at all, and her social behavior really reflected that.

I remember another moment, in the pouring rain in Hyde Park, when Pavarotti was singing for an audience. Diana went up to him in a design of mine, a double-breasted suit consisting of a jacket and skirt. She was absolutely soaked and she was beautifully suntanned. To me, the most radiant photograph of her that has ever appeared anywhere was taken then. If you ever get a chance to look at it, you must. It is featured in a couple of books about her. It really is something special to me—I have it on my wall, in my studio, at this very moment. Whenever I look at it, I get a lump in my throat.

There was another occasion when she wore something of mine that stands out in my mind. Diana was wearing a very sheer skirt and jacket and was standing in the sun. She was in India, in front of the Taj Mahal, and her skirt was see-through. Of course, the press went full out on that.

My last memory of her is when she was wearing a linen dress of mine in Melbourne and was surrounded by a large group of Australian swimmers. That, for me, was a very exciting moment.

She was always incredibly polite, incredibly generous. There is simply no comparison. She had a completely different manner from everyone else. I have been to Buckingham Palace, and she was always far above the rest. I must have been the one and only Irishman ever to dress a member of the Royal Family!

TESSA DAHL

❧

A daughter of famed British novelist Roald Dahl, Tessa Dahl was a good friend of Diana's and her colleague at several successful charities. A prolific writer and editor, Tessa is a regular contributor to many important British newspapers and magazines, including the *Sunday Times*, the *Daily Mail*, the *Telegraph*, *Vogue*, and the *Tatler*.

*T*he first time I met Diana was during an evening dinner party, at Prince and Princess Michael of Kent's.

Actually, this is not at all true.

My parents, Patricia Neal and Roald Dahl, were very close friends with Diana's aunt, Mary Berry. Mary was Diana's mother's sister and was married to a rather grand Conservative minister, Tony Berry.

We were about five, six, and seven when we used to have our bucket and spade holidays at the Berrys' Welsh seaside mansion.

By strange coincidence, a couple of years later when my mother had her strokes the year after she won best actress for *Hud,* we were invited to stay with Ethel and Bobby Kennedy at Hickory Hill, on our way back from Los Angeles, when we were bringing Mummy home to England. I was nine. I struck up a friendship with Courtney Kennedy, and we had a very scary competition about whose family had had more tragedies (this was just before Robert was shot). Years later, we became friends again and admitted to each other that we remembered the competition. It was eerily similar to my early friendship with Diana, which developed again when she was newly wed (yet, sadly, not very happy).

Of course, since our seaside holidays with the Spencers and the Berrys, Diana's mother had gone through her blood-curdling divorce. Once again, from my generation, I knew more children that were brought up as "nanny children" because the British courts seemed to deem that if a mother could leave her children, they were better being brought up by nannies (under the guise of their father) than the adulteress mother.

Anyway, before all the unhappiness, the Berrys had a beautiful Georgian home, at the edge of the white sand on the sea in South Wales. Diana was my age, and we got on as the best of friends. I remember we were a naughty couple. We would raise our eyes at each other as our parents got increasingly drunk, or whisper together about the terrifying arguments they would have of an early evening. We also shared the fact that our fathers were more hands on, although in reality the grown-ups were so narcissistic and involved in their own little affairs and affectations that it was really only in the nursery that our whisperings could be spoken.

After all, we did not eat dinner with our parents. Or, indeed, breakfast. Our mothers would have trays in bed and our fathers would eat kedgeree and read the newspapers in the dining room. We would have had our boiled eggs and be out, already dressed and catching sea crabs, before they were even up.

So, back to the evening we re-met, years later at the Kents'. Prince and Princess Michael of Kent were hosting a charity dinner. Most of their charity dinners were for themselves, so, quite honestly, I am not sure why Diana and I were guests. As the Prince and the Princess moved around, being gracious to their guests, I caught the Princess of Wales's eye. She was stifling a giggle. From that second, I knew I had an ally, as neither of us thought much of Princess Michael.

We then worked extensively for the charity Birthright. Diana was the patron and I was, for want of a better word, the "research arm." I suppose that she knew that there was no mucking about with me, and also perhaps saw a kindred spirit when it came to eating problems—we were the same size, seemed to use the same designers, and had tons of friends in common and dysfunctional families. We were both of shredding-machine skinniness. We would have countless encounters, mainly involving the charity. I think we also shared a passion for it because we loved our George Pinker (the royal gynecologist) and would have done anything for him. He wanted us to put our backs into the less glamorous. The charity dealt with incontinence, infertility, and recurrent miscarriages, and also the very scary, much-ignored problem of child abuse. The realities were that so much was now being done for infertility that often when a much-awaited, much-longed-for baby arrived, the ecstasy would be outweighed by the overwhelming anticlimax and exhaustion. We worked hard and she truly cared, as did I.

The Princess then chose me to host and organize a huge black-tie event at the London Palladium on behalf of Birthright to celebrate fifty years of *Woman* magazine, our version of *Good Housekeeping*. Although there were many dramas during the planning, the event was thrilling, and Richard Barbour, the editor of *Woman,* told me, "Hush; just absorb it." He was right.

When the Princess arrived, I made the introductions, which were such fun, although my hair was falling down . . . according to the photos. So I sat in the Royal Box next to her, and then we went to the Royal Loo (wooden seat) and I said to her, "How, ma'am, do you manage to go to the loo with such control; that is, not need to be rushing there all the time?" She replied that if you were due to attend a long function, you simply had to limit your liquids earlier, and then when you went to make sure you absolutely had totally, totally finished. Sorry, but I find these hints fascinating.

The only part that marred that night was, *typically,* my dad, Roald Dahl, who left at the interval. I was devastated, but that was his modus operandi. I wanted him to see me in the Royal Box. I fear most of the post-party was spent with me on the phone crying to him, after Diana had left and we had done the royal lineup. Gosh, she was always so good at that. Talk about doing her homework. Every single performer, she had time for, even knowing a little bit about each one.

We didn't see each other again until Bruce Oldfield's ball. Diana had come with Prince Charles and looked really miserable. Beautiful, in a gold gown (with Joan Collins trying to outdo her—good luck, Joan), but still, she had a new aura of hopelessness. Although she did dance with Bruce to KC and the Sunshine Band's "That's the Way I Like It." We stopped to talk. "How's Daisy?" she asked kindly. She obviously knew that I had been having my baby down the hall in the same hospital and at the same time as she had had Prince Harry. "Actually, it's a different bovine name. She's called Clover." I was touched that she had remembered that we had had our babies around the same time and that my little girl did have a good old-fashioned cow's name. I asked, "Wasn't it fun at the Lindo? I do love having babies." "I'm afraid I find it rather disgusting," she revealed. This, of course, was the famous time when Prince Charles had been so disparaging about Harry's being a redhead.

After that, one saw less of her. The final event she carried out for Birthright was a massive Red and Gold Ball we had at the Albert Hall. I worked ceaselessly on it. We had arranged at her request to have the Three Degrees sing, as we knew Prince Charles loved them. It really was to be a hugely grand affair, and at the time we did not realize that it was to be her Birthright swan song.

Meanwhile, I had been trying to get pregnant again, and being a recurrent miscarrier, I always had to treat myself during the "perhaps pregnant" times with kid gloves. Anyway, the day before the ball, I got a call from Vivian Parry, the lady who ran Birthright, saying, "The Princess of Wales wants you to sit next to Prince Charles."

Cool, I thought.

The next day (the day of the ball) I had that women's intuition that I might be pregnant and that if I was I was perhaps getting ready to miscarry, so I called George Pinker, who knew how hard I had worked for this event. A woman came to my house and did an instant blood test. Yes, I was pregnant. Then came actions and reactions that could only have happened in England. There I was . . . going to sit next to Prince Charles in the Royal Box at the Royal Albert Hall and risk having a miscarriage. Or I could put on my nightdress and go to bed.

The consensus that afternoon was hysterical. "Well, she wanted you to sit next to Prince Charles because she knows he likes tall, decent-looking, very funny ladies, so you have a dilemma," I was informed. I do not have a dilemma, I thought. I want to have another baby. Sure, I want to sit next to Prince Charles in the Royal Box, at the Red and Gold Ball that I have worked my balls off for—but one of our causes is recurrent miscarriage (I had already had four miscarriages and Clover had lost her twin) and I want a baby more than I want to sit next to Prince Charles.

I put away my dress and put on my nightie.

The next day, a huge, beautiful arrangement of flowers arrived. The message read: "You were sorely missed last night and we hope these flowers will cheer you up a little bit. Love, Diana." I thought they were from another Diana (Diana Donovan), who had ended up sitting next to Prince Charles. I called the florist.

"I know two Dianas," I said. "Which have they come from?"

"Kensington Palace," said the florist.

"Oh, that Diana," I said

Later, once my baby was firmly enmeshed, my husband and I were asked to dinner at Kensington Palace as a lovely treat. I think it was a lot more intimate, fun, and revealing than it would ever have been in the Royal Box at the Albert Hall.

I then got divorced. Diana and I had married the same year. We would see each other at parties, but she was changing. As was I. I was no longer a committee-woman who wore shoulder pads. I had written my first novel, but was fighting a terrible black Vulcan of depression that finally, after many years, revealed itself to be bipolar disorder. The death of my father had taken a violent hold on me. I had had an older sister called Olivia who had died of measles encephalitis she had caught from me. I was six, she was seven. She was the love of my father's life. He always blamed me for her death and had made it clear that it would have been far better had it been me. Thus, I had spent all my years trying to prove my worth to him. He was my entire motivation. Every breath I took was in the hope that somehow he would be proud of me. I had a very different childhood from my siblings because once I had been pushing the baby carriage with my nanny in New York City with my tiny baby brother in it when a taxi shot through the light, struck it, and threw it against a wall while I watched his tiny body bounce off a bus. He was left severely brain damaged.

Anna Freud had told Dad that we all needed counseling, but he refused (he was convinced it stopped you from being a good writer). Instead, from the time I was three and a half (when Theo's accident happened), Dad simply insisted on keeping me medicated. Anna Freud had refused, but there is *always* a doctor who will write a prescription. I was put on phenobarbital, and by the time my mama had her three strokes, I was eight and had graduated to being doctored by the phenobarbital during the day and barbiturates at night. So I never knew how to feel a feeling. Once Dad died, my entire world collapsed, because I had been keeping myself going by trying to win the unattainable. I had existed for him, and believe me, he may have been a great children's writer, but he did this child few favors. Nevertheless, I will always forgive him, and think he knew no better. He had a broken heart, and I was not good enough to mend it. You cannot live up to a dead sister. Especially one you think you killed. My siblings, however, never knew Olivia or Theo before his accident or Mum before her strokes. My father told me for the first and only time the night before he died that he loved me.

So I was pretty fragile and sliding down black ice.

At around this time Diana gave her amazingly brave *Panorama* interview on television about her problems. I related to it and respected her, and wrote her a letter that included my favorite poem, "After a While," by Veronica A. Shoffstall. Within a day, Diana wrote me a beautiful (as always) handwritten letter that read:

> *My dear Tessa,*
>
> Thank you for your wise, kind words and poem from a great lady who had travelled far. . . . It is up to those women such as us, who have a voice to help those poor ladies who do not.
>
> I will be away. When I return we should see what we can REALLY do.
>
> *Love, Diana*

Within five days, I had made a serious suicide attempt. I was not found (I had not intended to be found) for twenty hours and had been in a coma. The result—I was in a wheelchair being told that I would never walk again. I was by then firmly locked up in Payne Whitney in New York City.

Within another week, Diana was dead.

Today I walk. I am very well. I am writing my second novel. I am glad I am alive.

COLLEEN DENNEY, PhD

As professor of art history and adjunct in women's studies and African American studies at the University of
Wyoming, Colleen Denney studies Diana and her portraits as a scholar and an admirer. She is the author of
*Representing Diana, Princess of Wales: Cultural Memory
and Fairy Tales Revisited*, published in 2005.

I have worked on images of Diana for more
than seven years now, publishing a book
on her portraits in 2005. In the course of my work,
many people have sent me Diana memorabilia: a sou-
venir spoon with her young face on it, found in a flea
market in Holland; the Ron Bell engagement portrait
on a book of matches sold at the royal wedding itself.
These images sealed her fate as the fairy tale princess,
docile and passive. And for a long time she was simply
that image, the Princess of Wales of public and state
duty, getting on with the business of the job, gracious,
always funny.

But Diana became much more than that postcard
cutout persona once she realized she was worth more
than the commodity she had become. My students

71

found in her struggles fodder for discussions of the rebellious woman, the one who had the guts, the nerve, to stand up to the monarchy and find her own voice. The students who identified with her most were my nontraditional women students who themselves had faced personal trials. For them, and for me as a feminist, her fight against the establishment, her work for AIDS and against land mines, has empowered other women, given them the opportunity to address and redress their own inadequate lives, to face their own dilemmas and find their own voices.

I am currently working on other scandalous women—women who choose their own paths, such as the ninteenth-century suffragists—although Diana is probably the best example. What both compels me and repels me in my study of them is their acceptance of the necessity for a prim public persona that fits with the culture's ideal of womanhood. Contrary to that persona, the Diana who appeared in Mario Testino's photographs for *Vanity Fair* in 1997 was powerful—perhaps too powerful. She showed that a woman could be sexy and successful; as many women know, such a projection of self takes a fine balance.

I am a reader of memoirs and a sometimes writer of them. It was clear to me from a very young age that we should keep secrets; there was some instinct in me that said what to reveal, what to conceal, sparing others if not myself.

As I grew older, it became crystal clear to me that I had to project a public self very different from who I was in those memoirs, in those many journals that sit in a high stack in my study even today. It is best not to show any signs of vulnerability in that public self, not to allow any way for folks to get inside that private self; one must wear more armor, as Diana did. It is a depressing, but realistic, view to say that such an act is a matter of sheer survival. There's something ill begotten in human nature that is too ready to pounce on weakness, to single out the less-able elements, especially if the subject is a woman.

And yet, I think what Diana's defiance has taught us is that showing your vulnerability, laying yourself bare before others, can sometimes unnerve them and give you the upper hand. I like to imagine that that's how Diana and the other scandalous women I am studying came to think of their public selves, as ones more sharp-edged, calculated, and clearly articulated than those private selves they kept for home, husbands, lovers, children.

At some point in their lives, all of these women—like Diana, like my women students, my girlfriends, and myself—had to learn to leap off the text pages that men had written for them without their consent, because of circumstance, opportunity, talent, or utter will and desire. The Testino photographs of Diana, taken a few months before her death, offer us a way of explaining that journey and the crucial steps along its way.

DHARMENDRA

An accomplished actor and producer who has appeared in many Hindi films in India since the sixties, Dharmendra is also active in Indian politics. For his extensive and important contributions to Indian cinema over the years, Dharmendra was recently awarded the Filmfare Lifetime Achievement Award.

*P*rincess Diana was a very giving person and will never be forgotten for all that she has done. Not many people can maintain an open heart and a deep sensitivity to people's suffering in spite of their high positions.

Diana's concern for the people of the world and causes of real importance was heartfelt and genuine, and her dedication to the people, despite the enormous obstacles and limitations she faced, was truly admirable. She will be always be remembered for the compassion and humanity she showed toward the victims of the Angola land mines.

Princess Diana was a daughter of the soil, born with a silver spoon. Destiny made her a part of the Royal Family. This daughter of the soil felt herself to be a stranger among them, and that is the reason she was drawn back to the roots and started involving herself for the cause of the needy. In spite of being in the castle of royalty, she remained a very open person. She was unable to confine herself to being a member of the royalty. She started sharing the pain of the common people and touched every such heart with her humility and humanity.

My heart always had an urge to meet her and share my feelings with her, since I, too, am a son of the soil. It is very unfortunate that I was unable to meet her personally, but I will always cherish the memory of her. Her death was very unfortunate and untimely and affected millions of people all over the world, including me. To me, she was a kindred spirit, and I felt at one with her for her compassion and generosity.

NORA DUNN

Nora Dunn is an American actress and comedian best known for her extensive work on NBC's *Saturday Night Live*. She is also a former member of the famed *Second City* comedy troupe in Chicago, where she met many comedians who would later become superstars on television and in Hollywood. Recognized for her exceptional impersonations, Dunn was instrumental in revitalizing *Saturday Night Live* during the late 1980s.

When Princess Diana was killed, I was in the middle of a run of a one-woman show. I had no idea of the effect she'd had on me until I got that news. It was eerie to watch the ambulance at the accident scene, and strange, I think, that they did not rush her to a hospital sooner. Though I'd never met her, I had felt for her, and her treatment in death seemed as shoddy and unfair as it had been in life. She was a starry-eyed girl who fell in love with a prince who didn't love her back. I admit I was one of those who shared her indignation and felt her pain. Her humiliation was public, and she was flagrantly unprotected. Of course her behavior was embarrassing. Of course her desperation made me cringe. But in the end, she rescued herself from the castle, by herself and with no knight in shining armor. For that achievement alone, she has my loyalty for life. Up against the most powerful in-laws in the world, she outplayed them brilliantly.

I stayed up all night watching Princess Diana's funeral and wept through her brother's eulogy. And like a starstruck teen, I secretly dedicated all my remaining shows to her memory. Her fate still makes me wistful. She was an ordinary woman caught in an extraordinary circumstance. She was naive and girlish, and she wasn't cynical enough not to be devastated by her husband's betrayal. When faced with no real friends, she went out into the world and made some, and to watch her try to create a life with meaning was touching.

Although she exposed the foolishness of a monarchy, she also made it work. The weight of her nobility played outside the boundaries of lineage. Her penchant to reach out to lost souls was real, and when the pundits diminished her in death, and expressed puzzlement at how many had been affected by her, their cynicism served only to reaffirm her vulnerability. In life, her loneliness was palpable; in death, she created a stillness, I think. We took pause. The fact that I did not know her did not make my sadness any less heartfelt. She was an icon, but her allure was not her great sense of style, though her style and her great looks were fun to watch. Indeed, when considering Paris Hilton (if I must), there is no hint of likeness here. Diana's taste was classic and her search for self was sweet. Her appeal and her endurance in death is that she so publicly endeavored to find true love. In that regard she had no conceit, and has no equal. I loved her because, unlike any other icon, she was so acutely human.

RICHARD, EARL OF BRADFORD

☙

Richard, the seventh Earl of Bradford, is an experienced and reputable restaurateur. Also an author and an Internet business owner, Lord Bradford is the proprietor of Weston Park, a beautiful estate in Shropshire. As president of the Foundation for Conductive Education in Birmingham from 1991 to 1994, Lord Bradford worked closely with Diana, who was patron of the foundation at that time.

*F*rom 1991 to 1994, I was president of the Stepping Stones Appeal for the Foundation for Conductive Education in Birmingham. Explained very simply, we ran a clinic for adults and children who were suffering either from cerebral palsy or were brain damaged in some way, and, by using techniques pioneered by the Peto Institute in Hungary, improved their quality of life, sometimes enabling children to go into the normal educational system, rather than having to attend special schools.

During that time, Princess Diana was our patron and helped us enormously, partly with the fund-raising, but also by increasing the profile of the great work that was being carried out; she normally set aside three occasions a year when she would help us in one way or another.

Sometimes that might be a fund-raising lunch in London. We once held one at the Carlton Towers Hotel, where I had the great pleasure of sitting next to her.

Normally, members of the Royal Family, even those that have married into it, tend to have a stiffness and formality about their behavior, creating a rather stultified atmosphere at any event attended by them. Not so with Princess Diana, who made everyone feel relaxed, and laughed along with the rest of us.

She also had a special, almost incandescent quality to her, and on various occasions when she was present at an event, I could see the effect that she had on all who met her.

However, the highlight for us was when she came to Birmingham to visit the institute. It was then that her caring character came to the fore. At that difficult and stressful time, it would have been possible to view every public appearance by her as an opportunity for her to boost her popularity; but when she came to the institute, she met everybody involved as she arrived, but then chose to spend most of her time with the children, watching them being taught the techniques that would help them to lead a normal life.

There were journalists and photographers present in droves when she arrived—naturally, they all wanted to cover her visit—but the only photo opportunity that she provided for them was outside the center, never when she was inside.

The greatest legacy that she has left is the two young princes. Despite the pressure that has been upon them, they are wonderfully normal and she must be delighted at the way they have turned out.

BARBARA EDEN

⚜

Primarily known as the star of the classic 1960s sitcom *I Dream of Jeannie*, Barbara Eden remains one of television's most distinguished and identifiable figures. Her feature film credits are also extensive, including *Flaming Star* in 1960, *The Brass Bottle* in 1964, and *Harper Valley PTA* in 1978. She has starred opposite many of Hollywood's most famous leading men, Elvis Presley and Tony Randall among them.

was always very impressed that Princess Diana spent so much of her time helping people. Right up to the end of her life, she was involved with charities that helped children, the homeless, AIDS victims, and many others. I never got the chance to meet her, but I do remember feeling an admiration and kind of love when I'd see her on the news visiting children's hospitals and talking about the urgent need to find and destroy land mines. In a way, we all got to be with her in spirit when she appeared on TV at these events. She was very real, but also a little bit magical, like an angel moving around the world helping people wherever she went. And we got to see her children, Prince William and Prince Harry, grow up to young manhood. I know they were very proud of their famous beautiful mom, as I'm sure she was of them. Surely, she was an inspiration to all of us, everywhere. And it may not be generally known, but Diana donated to charity many dresses she had worn on important occasions so they could be sold to raise funds for the needy. She had impeccable taste in her clothes, which often were copied and began global fashion trends of their own, helping the careers of many young British designers.

I felt so sad when she announced in a TV interview that she and Prince Charles were getting divorced. My heart went out to her. And when I heard about her death, it seemed unbelievable, as if the news were wrong and we would soon hear it corrected. Her last official engagement in Britain, I understand, was—quite typically—at the children's accident and emergency unit in London's Northwick Park Hospital, visiting little boys and girls, trying to ease their discomfort, even if only for a little while.

Diana died at a very young thirty-six. She gave much of her life to charities to help so many people. Representatives of these charities were given the honor of walking with Diana's family behind her coffin from

St. James's Palace to Westminster Abbey on the day of her funeral. We cannot help but wonder what might have been, how much more she might have accomplished, if granted a different destiny.

MEREDITH
ETHERINGTON-SMITH

Meredith Etherington-Smith became an editor of Paris *Vogue* in London and GQ magazine in the United States during the 1970s. During the 1980s, she served as deputy and features editor of *Harpers & Queen* magazine and has since become a leading art critic. Currently, she is editor in chief of *Christie's* magazine. She is also a noted artist biographer; her book on Salvador Dalí, *The Persistence of Memory,* was an international bestseller and was translated into a dozen languages.

The first time I met Princess Diana, it was to discuss putting on a sale of her "state" dresses at Christie's. I was asked to go to Kensington Palace one sunny morning in September 1996. At the time, the Princess, recently divorced, was beginning a new life pursuing her charitable instincts and wanted to sell the dresses to raise money for AIDS and cancer-research causes.

Her drawing room that morning was much like any comfortable, slightly formal drawing room to be found in country houses throughout England: the paintings, hung on pale yellow walls, were better; the furniture, chintz-covered; the flowers, natural garden bouquets. It was charming. And so was she, as she swooped in from a room beyond. I had never seen pictures of her without any makeup, with just-washed hair and dressed in jeans and a white T-shirt. She looked more vital, more beautiful, than any photograph had ever managed to convey. She was, in a word, staggering; here was the most famous woman in the world up close, relaxed, funny, and warm. The tragic Diana, the royal Diana, the wronged Diana, vanished. In their place, I found a different Diana: a clever, interesting person who wasn't afraid to say she didn't know how an auction sale worked, and would it be possible to work with me on it?

"Of course, ma'am," I said. "It's your sale, and if you would like, then we'll work on it together to make the most money we can for your charities." "So what do we do next?" she asked me. "First, I think you had better choose the clothes for sale." The next time I saw her drawing room, Paul Burrell, her butler, had wheeled in rack after rack of jeweled, sequined, embroidered, and lacy dresses, almost all of which I recognized from photographs of the Princess at some state event or gala evening. The visible relics of a royal life that had ended.

The Princess, in another pair of immaculately pressed jeans and a stripy shirt, looked so different from these formal meringues that it was almost laughable. I think at that point the germ of an idea entered my mind: that sometime, when I had gotten to know her better and she trusted me, I would like to see photographs of the "new" Princess Diana—a modern woman unencumbered by the protocol of royal dress. Eventually, this idea led to putting together the suite of pictures of this sea-change princess with Mario Testino.

I didn't want her to wear jewels; I wanted virtually no makeup and completely natural hair. "But Meredith, I always have people do my hair and makeup," she explained. "Yes ma'am, but I think it is time for a change—I want Mario to capture your speed, and electricity, the real you and not the Princess." She laughed and agreed, but she did turn up at the historic shoot laden with her turquoise leather jewel boxes. We never opened them. Hair and makeup took ten minutes, and she came out of the dressing room looking breathtaking. The pictures are famous now; they caused a sensation at the time. My favorite memory of Princess Diana is when I brought the work prints round to Kensington Palace for her to look at. She was so keen to see them that she raced down the stairs and grabbed them. She went silent for a moment or two as she looked at these vivid, radiant images. Then she turned to me and said, "But these are really me. I've been set free and these show it. Don't you think," she asked me, "that I look a bit like Marilyn Monroe in some of them?" And laughed.

ROSIE FISHER
AND ADAM DALE

As founder and owner of Dragons of Walton Street, Rosie Fisher operates a unique and successful children's furniture store in London. Frequented by Diana during William and Harry's early years, Dragons of Walton Street and Rosie Fisher had the opportunity to design the Princes' earliest furniture. Benefiting from the work of Rosie and her associate, Adam Dale, along with eighteen highly skilled artists, Dragons continues to produce exquisite, handcrafted pieces for children.

*D*ragons of Walton Street, London, was lucky enough, in our early days, to receive an order for our then tiny Prince William's nursery. How exciting! What an honor. I was longing to shout it from the rooftops, but I was sworn to secrecy. Discretion was vital. The design we were to paint on the furniture was very appropriate as it depicted Prince Charles and Princess Diana's most loved hobbies. The design to this day is still a secret!

My best artist lovingly handpainted the items with extra-special care. A labor of love for our future king! It looked perfectly gorgeous, and I hoped that little

William would enjoy the pieces. Later, Princess Diana became a regular visitor to my showroom. Always arriving unannounced and behaving in the most natural of ways, she would leave her private detective in the car. One October, she came in clutching a big book full of the names and ages of her friends' children, godchildren, nieces, and nephews to buy their Christmas goodies. We would duly paint the presents and deliver them to Kensington Palace. Once she came into Dragons to talk about having chairs decorated for one of her godchildren, and while we were wrapping various other gifts she had chosen, she sat and chatted with us, confessing that one day she would love to have a little girl. I feel so sad that was never to be.

Diana

BY ADAM DALE

Beguiled by her innocence
Intrigued by her mystery
Bathed in her sunlight
Smiled at her triumphs
Cried at her anguish
Buoyed by her hope
Humbled by her greatness

Moved by her honesty
Heartened by her courage
Enveloped by her life
Dazzled by her beauty
Embraced by her love
Haunted by her tragedy
Emptied by her absence.

DANIEL GALVIN SR., OBE

Daniel Galvin Sr., OBE, is one of Britain's biggest names in hairdressing. His specialization in hair coloring has revolutionized the field over the past four decades, and he continues to be in high demand by the rich and famous worldwide. For his contributions to the industry, he was honored with an OBE in 2006.

I had the pleasure of knowing Diana and doing her hair color for ten years. She was truly a breath of fresh air each time she came into the salon. She was always happy, always full of life, and full of grace.

We have a private room available in our salon, but Diana never requested to use it. She was happy to sit next to other clients and often chatted away merrily with them and staff members.

In our business, confidentiality is so important. Anything she discussed with me will never go any further. She used to tell me off for my suntan—telling me it wasn't good for me and to be careful. Her last words to me before that tragic weekend in France were "Daniel, I don't believe it, but for the first time I'm browner than you!"

She was incredibly down-to-earth, unaffected, and perfectly charming on all occasions. She was a tremendous asset to the monarchy and to this country. There was an amazing aura that glowed around her—she was as beautiful on the inside as she was on the outside. It was always an honor to be of service to her.

SONIA GANDHI

Italian-born Indian politician Sonia Gandhi is the president of the Indian National Congress Party. Having entered politics after the death of her husband, former Indian prime minister Rajiv Gandhi, she has championed many humanitarian issues throughout her political career, including economic reform and the eradication of poverty.

*I*n India, the abiding memory of Princess Diana is of her genuine compassion and empathy for the marginalized.

Princess Diana's interactions with the underprivileged—be they slum children, AIDS victims, the physically or mentally challenged, or people on their deathbed—were always warm, direct, and human. She approached them unflinchingly, with love and humility, wanting to share their burden and deepen her own understanding of their deprivation and pain.

We remember Princess Diana, too, for her radiant beauty and grace, her vibrant natural charm, and the enthusiasm with which she embraced new experiences and encounters. These qualities enabled her to strike up an easy rapport with people from all cultures and walks of life, and left an indelible impression on those whose paths crossed hers even briefly.

TIM GRAHAM

❧

Tim Graham has specialized in photographing the Royal Family for more than thirty years and is foremost in his chosen field. Recognition of his work over the years has led to invitations for private sessions with almost all the members of the British Royal Family, including, of course, Diana, Princess of Wales, and her children.

My first picture of the Princess was taken one-on-one with her when she was the shy, nineteen-year-old Lady Diana Spencer. My "exclusive" session came about because I had arrived too late at the kindergarten where she worked to join a photo call that had been hastily arranged by the national newspapers as soon as news of her romance broke. She felt overwhelmed by the level of that first press attention, and the smile that could so readily light up her face, one that I was to see so many times over the coming years, was hidden that day.

While photographing the Princess over the years, I saw many contrasts. She could be regal and glamorous at a banquet, chatty while perching on a hospital patient's bed, at ease joking with celebrities at a pop concert. When she shook hands with leprosy sufferers and AIDS patients, she knew the resulting photographs would do much to overcome people's prejudices and help get those donations rolling in. Photographically, the body armor she wore in the Angolan minefields formed a dramatic contrast to the tiara and jewels she chose for state occasions. In every situation, she seemed confident and caring. Quite early on, people all over the world recognized something very special in her.

For at-home photographs, I found her chatty and easy to work with, and her sense of humor always showed through. Tours could be eventful. On one occasion, while photographing her at a Saudi Arabian desert picnic, I was walking backward in front of her—a position quite normal for photographers. What I didn't realize while concentrating on her was that I was backing straight into a fire. Just in time, the Princess called out to warn me, but couldn't suppress her giggles as I stepped into the flames.

She was a very lively person to photograph. You had to keep your camera on her at all times, because in a split second there could be just *the* picture of her expression or response to someone she was meeting or something that had happened. She had the ability to charm and relax whoever she met, whether the man in the street or a nation's president. If things went wrong in the job, it always made her laugh—and it's true to say that she must have found some of her royal duties a bit monotonous and stifling and been glad of some light relief.

Diana had none of the remoteness of some members of royal families. Along with several of my press colleagues, I felt I came to know her quite well. She was a superstar, she was royal, but she was also very approachable. I have had various sessions with members of the Royal Family over the years, but those with her were more informal. I remember photographing Prince William at Kensington Palace when he was a baby. I was lying on the floor of the drawing room in front of the infant prince, trying to get his attention. Not surprisingly, he didn't show much interest, so, without prompting, Diana lay down on the floor close to me and, using one of those little bottles of bubbles, started blowing bubbles at him. Perfect. As he gazed in fascination at his mother, I was able to get the picture I wanted. I can't think of many members of the Royal Family who would abandon protocol and lie on the carpet with you in a photo session!

Funnily enough, it wasn't the only time it happened. She did the same again years later when she was about to send her dresses to auction for charity and we were sifting through prints of my photographs that she had asked to use in the catalog. She suggested that we sit on the floor and spread the photographs all around us on the carpet, so, of course, we did.

I donated the use of my pictures of her in the various dresses to the charity, and as a thank-you, Diana invited me to be the exclusive photographer at both parties held for the dresses auction—one in London and the other in the United States. The party in New York was held on preview night, and many of the movers and shakers of New York were there, including her good friend Henry Kissinger. It was a big room, but everyone in it gravitated to the end where the Princess was meeting people. She literally couldn't move and was totally hemmed in. I was pushed so close to her I could hardly take a picture. Seeing the crush, her bodyguard spotted an exit route through the kitchen and managed to get the Princess and me out of the enthusiastic "scrum." As the kitchen door closed behind the throng, she leaned against the wall, kicked off her stiletto-heeled shoes, and gasped, "Gordon Bennett, that's a crush!" I would have loved to have taken a picture of her then, but I knew she wouldn't expect that to be part of the deal. You should have seen the kitchen staff—they were thrilled to have an impromptu sight of her but amazed that someone of her status could be so normal. She took a short breather, said hi to those who had, of course, stopped work to stare at her, and then glided back into the room through another door to take up where she had left off. That's style!

Her "magic" was a combination of style and compassion. She instinctively knew what was right for every occasion. One of my favorite photographs is a shot I took in Angola in 1997 that shows her with a young land-mine victim who had lost a leg. This image of the Princess was chosen by the Red Cross to appear on a poster to publicize the tragic reality of land mines. It's an important part of her legacy. It is difficult to capture such a remarkable person in just one photo, but I like this one a lot because it sums up her warmth and concern. Diana had one of those faces that would be very hard to photograph badly. Over the years, there were times when she was fed up or sad, and those emotions I captured, too. They were relevant at the time. I felt horrified by the news of her death and that she could die in such a terrible, simply tragic way. I couldn't conceive of how her sons would be able to cope with such a loss. I was asked just before the funeral to photograph Prince Charles taking William and Harry out in public for the first time so they could meet the crowds gathered at Kensington Palace and see the floral tributes. It was the saddest of occasions.

I had by then received an invitation to the funeral

and was touched to have been the only press photographer asked. After much deliberation, I decided to turn down the chance to be a guest in Westminster Abbey. Having photographed Diana for seventeen years, from the day she appeared as Prince Charles's intended, right through her public and, on occasion by invitation, her private life, I felt that I had to take the final picture. It was the end of an era. From my press position at the door of the abbey, I watched everyone arrive for the service, including my wife, who had also been invited. During my career, I have witnessed so many historic events from the other side of a camera that I felt compelled to take that last photograph of the Princess's story.

Life has moved on, and the public have found other subjects to fascinate them—not least the now grown-up sons of this international icon—but everyone knows Diana was unique.

JOAN HANGER

❧

Joan Hanger is the author of six books and a multimedia dream diva. She analyzes the dreams of celebrities for a number of publications, including Britain's *Closer Magazine* and *Daily Mirror* newspapers. She also maintains her website at www.joanhanger.com, and her latest book, *Diana's Dreams,* was published in London in October 2005. As Diana's friend and dream confidante, Joan helped the Princess through difficult and important times in her life.

It was a time when controversy was raging around the late Princess of Wales. Her marriage had reached a crisis point, and scandal erupted when Will Carling admitted to having had an affair with her. Despite the maelstrom raging around her, Diana invited me to Kensington Palace. The motivation was to support one of the Princess's favorite charities.

It felt like coming home—the car was parked in the drive, the door was ajar, and the welcome mat was out. But this was not my home—this was Kensington Palace, London. Before me were the private apartments of Her Royal Highness, the Princess of Wales, someone who, I would soon discover, was everything a dynamic young woman of the nineties should be.

Diana had already made the momentous decision that she would divorce Prince Charles, yet she gave no sign of a troubled mind. This was a princess graced with charm, elegance, and warmth—a proud young mother, a courageous champion of causes, a strikingly beautiful and energetic royal who took my breath away. But only for a moment.

Because one of the first things that happened in this woman's company was that you immediately forget to be overawed by who she really was—perhaps the most written-about woman of the last century.

I was there to seek her support for a project I was planning for the children's charity Barnardos Australia— a charity of which the Princess of Wales was royal president.

After our first meeting, I left not only with her support, but also with the feeling that I had made a lifelong friend.

My journey to Kensington Palace really began in May 1995 when I was a guest at the Stafford Hotel in St. James's Place during the Victory Day celebrations in London. I was at a formal dinner—a glittering affair with guests from around the world, including royalty, dignitaries, and celebrities, such as Paul Newman and his wife, Joanne Woodward. Outside, thousands were singing along to the strains of "Vera Lynn." All London was intoxicated with nostalgia.

By the end of that evening, I had a mission. It had been suggested that I make contact with the Buckingham Palace press office with a view to seeking a brief audience with the Princess of Wales. I knew of her affinity for children, and the project that had taken me to London was a children's book I was writing to raise funds for Barnardos Australia.

Little did I imagine the enthusiasm with which my idea would be greeted by the Princess. Yes, Diana was interested in meeting with me. Yes, I would be granted an audience. And yes, I had to pinch myself and can now admit that I never believed it would actually happen!

What do you wear to meet a princess? You don't wear your shabby chic, that's for sure! A quick shopping trip to London's Harrods and Harvey Nichols and I was transformed. No longer the look of the traveler— it was time for morning tea at the palace.

Wearing my new red two-piece woolen suit, my black fur-trimmed suede gloves, and my trusty black cashmere coat from New York, I felt I could handle anything.

It was 11:30 a.m. on a Friday. I had been given fifteen minutes to interview the Princess, but more than an hour later we parted warmly.

I was greeted at the door by a formally dressed young man called Paul—the butler. I was fractionally late, delayed by the heavy security surrounding London due to the recent bombings. My taxi had been eased through the security gates and stopped next to a shiny royal-blue BMW parked outside. I knew it belonged to the Princess.

Paul ushered me inside. Immediately, I felt welcome. I carried a bunch of violets I'd chosen as a gift for the Princess. Paul took my coat and gloves, then steered me through a doorway to a wide staircase, leading to the Princess's private apartment.

I stepped onto a beautiful carpet with green motifs, which led to the first level of the grand staircase. As we reached the top of that first level, I saw a large portrait of Diana. I remarked on how stunning it was, to which Paul replied, "I'm glad you like it—we love it. It's the latest portrait of Her Royal Highness, done by New York artist Norman Shanks last year."

As I turned, my eyes still on the picture, I sensed movement from above. I still couldn't see her, but I knew she was approaching. I felt incredibly excited. It was not so much nervousness as anticipation.

At the last step, I wondered, what should I do next? Curtsy? Genuflect? It didn't matter, because it was too late. She was there. I held out my hand. She took it warmly, smiling wonderfully. Then she spoke my name. I'd never liked it before. Suddenly, I loved it!

Thus began my memories of Diana. I met with her many times at her residence and also here in Australia when she visited. I helped her analyze her dreams. She was excited by this and enjoyed our chats on this subject, which we continued to have until her death.

I remember her glowing "peaches-and-cream" complexion.

I remember how her effusive mannerisms revealed her lovely natural spontaneity. Her spiritual awareness when she spoke of the many that she visited in hospitals and that needed her touch. Her amazing dream of her own funeral, which, at the time, I interpreted as the "death" of her marriage.

I remember her breathless, yet infectious laughter; her graceful energy when she moved; her sense of fun when her hands were held to her face in mock shock horror! Yet her seriousness was evident when we discussed subjects like her startling interview on *Panorama*.

All these memories and more make me enormously proud that I had the honor of feeling like a kindred spirit in the presence of this dynamic young woman—sharing her love of movies, like *Thelma & Louise,* sharing our love of our children, and ultimately sharing our love of life!

I look for Diana in my dreams now and, strangely enough for those who haven't yet tapped into their subconscious, I find her there, and that is my secret memory for myself!

NIGEL HAVERS

❧

One of Britain's leading stage and television actors, Nigel Havers has also appeared in many outstanding film productions, including *Chariots of Fire*, *A Passage to India*, *Empire of the Sun*, *The Whistle Blower*, *Farewell to the King*, *Quiet Days in Clichy*, and *The Private War of Lucinda Smith*. He has recently completed his autobiography, *Playing with Fire*, published by Headline.

*D*iana and I first met properly when I was doing some PR stuff for Dunhill. They had asked me to be a sort of clotheshorse for a shoot for the *Daily Telegraph* and wanted to use an actor, not a model. Instead of payment, they said they would supply me with clothes, which was fine, as I love their stuff. Shortly afterward, they rang me and said, "I understand you are going to a charity bash tonight and we see from the list Princess Diana is also going. As it is her birthday the following day, would you present her with a Dunhill watch for us?"

They knew that if Diana wore one of their watches, it would be terrific PR, and so they gave me one from their newest line, beautifully wrapped in a presentation case. As luck would have it, I was seated next to Diana at the dinner, and Paul McCartney was on her other side. I had Linda McCartney on my left. During the evening, Linda told me that she had never read a book in her life, that the only books she ever picked up were cookbooks, which I found extraordinary. Paul was a bit odd, too, and Diana seemed more than anxious to chat with me, which delighted me. As soon as the opportunity arose, I turned to her and said with a grand gesture: "I know it's your birthday tomorrow—here is a present." And with that, I pressed the beautifully wrapped box into her hand.

She opened it straight away, and when she saw the watch she was all over me.

"Oh my God," she said, "I love it!" And on it went. It was a very nice watch—gold and lovely—and she wore it for years. She obviously thought I had bought it for her, because she wrote me a wonderful, gushing thank-you letter. I wrote back, and so we started a correspondence. We wrote to each other quite a lot, and I have kept all the letters, which were funny and charming. I fancied her hugely, of course, and would have leaped into bed with her given half a chance, but it never happened—and if it had, I would never have told anyone. My father (Attorney General Sir Michael Havers) had different ideas—he had convinced himself I was having an affair with her. He would walk around his club—the Garrick—telling anyone who cared to listen that his son and Diana were having an affair! It was completely out of order. But it was just Dad at the Garrick.

Anyway, I remember another occasion at Wimbledon, when it was the men's finals. At the time, Dad was not only the MP for Wimbledon but also the attorney general, so as a family we were given two tickets for every match. Dad was in the Royal Box with Mum and invited me and Caro (my wife at the time) for tea in the Royal Box afterward. When we arrived, there was Princess Diana, who was all over me like a cheap suit and completely ignored Caro. I could see that this was doing nothing to dispel Dad's idea that we were having an affair, and then to cap it all Diana turned to me coyly and—I remember her words very well—said, "What does one do when this is all over? [Meaning the tennis.] Go home and watch a blue movie?"

I could see Dad's eyebrows twitching, and I replied weakly, "I suppose one does."

I realized Diana loved to shock—it was her way of flirting—and because she was who she was, she got away with saying the most outrageous things.

When I separated from Caro and was with Polly (who eventually became my second wife), Diana wrote to me and said she was sorry to hear about all my problems, but she was so glad I had somebody else. When Dad died, the first letter I got was from her. By that time, I had bought a flat in Sheffield Terrace, which was only a stone's throw from Kensington Palace, and Diana wrote and asked if she could come to tea. I was working and living on my own in the flat as Polly was in the country, so it was Diana and me. She would walk over from Kensington Palace to see me. We would talk for ages about everything—her children and my marriage. I would tell her about how difficult my life had become as I had fallen in love with someone else and felt so guilty about leaving my wife and daughter. We had these sorts of marriage discussions for hours, and I used to fantasize about going upstairs to get something and coming downstairs again and there she would be—completely naked. But that never happened, of course.

I felt she was rather like a marriage counselor with me. She didn't say much about herself; she wanted to listen to me, and just kept saying her marriage was very difficult. I found myself telling her everything, as I trusted her completely. She obviously had her friends, and Prince Charles had his. She kept on telling me how lonely her marriage was and how people always thought they were very busy, but in fact they weren't very busy at all. They didn't do much apart from the public things together. They didn't do any fun things together like go to great weekend country house parties. I felt really sorry for her. She was incredibly beautiful one-on-one. The way she looked at you and that honey skin took my breath away.

Years before, when she and Prince Charles had come to the *Chariots of Fire* premiere, she had the same effect on me. It was also the first time she met Dodi Al Fayed, who had financed the movie. I became a great friend of Dodi's, and he was a most adorable man, but a bit feckless in a way. He didn't seem to have much direction. He disappeared after the first day of filming of *Chariots* and never came back until we hauled it in. But he was a lovely man.

So Diana and I had this funny relationship. Polly was very wary of her and kept saying how dangerous she was, describing to me how Diana would get her claws into a married man and bombard him with phone calls, but she certainly never did that to me. Just sent me lots of lovely letters. Polly did get hold of them once, as I used to keep them at Sheffield Terrace, but they were innocent, so that was fine.

One afternoon, when I was filming a series called *The Good Guys* and Polly was away in Spain, all the crew were all a bit beady-eyed with me.

"What on earth is going on, guys?" I asked. But they kept looking at me in a strange way.

It transpired that on the front of the *Evening Standard* was the first transcript of the Diana tapes—the Squidgy tapes—and no one knew who the man calling Diana Squidgy was and the headline on the front page said it was me! As everyone was hiding the paper from me, I went and grabbed it.

"My God, it's not me. It's not me, I know," I said.

It wasn't me, of course. But when you read something and your name is in banner headlines, there is a split second when you almost believe it. I called Diana at once (she had given me her private mobile number), and she laughed like a drain when I told her how panicked I was. She literally couldn't stop laughing.

I was a bit jumpy around her because I fancied her so much, but I really just felt sad for her. When she came to tea with me, she would be wearing jeans and a T-shirt. She just walked out of Kensington Palace and up Kensington High Street to my flat. She told me that no one would turn around, and as they weren't expecting to see her strolling down the street, she was never recognized.

Ten years ago I was on a plane, off to LA to do a film for HBO. My agent failed to collect me from the airport, so I had to get a cab. It was a nightmare, as the cabs are appalling and haven't a clue where to go. I asked the driver—who spoke no known language—to take me to the Four Seasons Hotel. So there I am on the way to the Four Seasons and the cabdriver said in a thick accent, "She didn't make it."

I said, "What?" He repeated, "Princess Diana didn't make it." I thought she hadn't made the flight. Oh damn, she might have been on the same flight as me!

When I finally arrived at the hotel and checked in, the first thing they said to me was "Did you hear about Princess Diana—she didn't make it." Then they told me she was dead. That was how I found out. When I hear people are dead, I always think it's not possible. I was in shock.

When I arrived back in England, Polly and I picked flowers from our garden in Barnes and we walked all the way to Kensington Palace and put them outside with the 25 million others. That was my sort of gesture to her.

The world is a grayer place without her. She was good to me, and I hope I might have helped her a bit, but I had trouble dragging things out of her because she didn't want to talk about herself. I suppose at the time my troubles seemed as bad as hers, and it was part of her character that she was able to deal with other people's problems far better than she could her own.

PATRICK JEPHSON

꙳

As the first and only private secretary to Diana during her life, Patrick Jephson was one of the closest people to the Princess throughout her international charity and diplomatic career. He is also a notable broadcaster and journalist and has contributed to many major British newspapers, including the *Times*, the *Observer*, and the *Daily Mail*. His writing credits include *Shadows of a Princess* and *Portraits of a Princess: Travels with Diana*, and several of his books have been international bestsellers.

Twenty-five years ago the House of Windsor metaphorically tapped its loyal subjects on the shoulder and invited them to welcome Diana Spencer into their collective life. Such a royal wish was easy to obey—Prince Charles's photogenic young fiancée seemed just the sort of new recruit the monarchy needed. So welcome her they did, with an enthusiasm that must have delighted the royal strategists. Hundreds of thousands duly celebrated the fairy-tale wedding that would secure the monarchy far into the future.

Having been invited, many of us continued to keep

Diana in our lives. This was perhaps easier for me because she actually employed me for a large chunk of mine. Traveling around the world with her, I realized that people liked her so much that for many she became almost an extra member of the family. An exasperating one at times, it's true, but one who somehow always earned our forgiveness. This reaction wasn't just sentimental, however beguiling her blue eyes sometimes seemed. There was steel in Her Royal Highness, the Princess of Wales, and it was as much by her guts as her uncanny ability to spread hope and happiness that she earned that forgiveness.

Not everybody's forgiveness, of course. There was (and is) a powerful minority who found it hard to rejoice at her popularity. They suspected her motives and resented her success at carving out a role as a glamorous worldwide force for good.

Most of these Diana skeptics confined their criticism to disapproving mutterings in smart addresses in London and the English shires. A few allowed their unattributable gripes to appear in sympathetic establishment newspapers. But such knavish tricks were usually confounded. Criticizing Diana only seemed to make her a more sympathetic figure, especially once it was known that her husband had a nonnegotiable arrangement with Mrs. Parker Bowles. Diana's own un-happiness and misjudgments just seemed to make her more intuitive at understanding our own.

So when, only sixteen short years after we had been asked to welcome her, we were unexpectedly asked to say good-bye, millions felt a bereavement so strong that it became indelibly marked on our memory. Diana came into our lives as our future queen, not as a soap star. That alone makes her worth remembering—and worth respecting, too, as the Queen eloquently demon-strated when she opened the Diana Memorial.

As a nation, the British like to remember things, especially things that make them feel special. Trying to forget Diana is a tall order—and not just for those of us who knew her well. What happened to her dur-ing those sixteen years was drama on a Shakespearean scale—just think of love, betrayal, sacrifice, beauty, and death. The curtain may have come down on the trag-edy ten years ago. But our farewell to Diana is not yet complete. It probably never will be.

It's a memory that is renewed each time we see a photograph of her sons. William in particular carries the blessing (or the burden) of Diana's camera-friendly looks. Her DNA in our future heads of state is now an ineradicable biological fact. Time may fade that reality. But nobody can deny it.

So when you hear people moan that the Diana story has outstayed its welcome, pause to consider what they really mean. Are they saying the Diana tragedy has no lessons for the future conduct of the Royal Family? Or is it just that the lessons are too painful to contemplate? Diana is unlikely to fade away while her sad experience still has the power to raise awkward questions like these. The good news is that if they are prepared to look, the people who live and work in palaces may find Diana's ghost does more than frisk along those deeply carpeted corridors. It may have a lesson to pass on . . .

Her critics would argue that "caring Di" was in fact "flaky Di"—an unstable airhead, a clotheshorse with a disarming smile that hid a vicious temper. One of Charles's favored biographers was even encouraged to diagnose her as suffering from mental illness. The implication was that everybody had tried their best, but really, the girl was *impossible* . . . so no one's really to blame.

And as I discovered to my cost, the image of the compassionate princess was not always kept up behind the scenes. Diana did have a temper, and she wasn't always entirely rational about where she aimed it. She could be tetchy, scheming, and unreasonable. But from my position as her most senior adviser I could clearly see that even on a bad day she usually gave far more—

to her country, her family, and her staff—than she took for herself.

Her appeal in the long run owes more to perceptions of honesty and sacrifice than to touchy-feely superficiality. Mistimed they may sometimes have been and embarrassing, too, but her attempts to turn her predicament to good use were genuine. The duty to be honest was more important to her than the duty to keep silent. For many of her critics, that was at best an indulgence and at worst an unforgivable sin. If it was either, she certainly paid a high price for it.

Her undoubted concern would be that nobody has to pay such a high price in the future. Most especially not her sons. They are her living legacy, and if there are lessons to be learned from her life, it is they who have the most to gain by recognizing them.

So let's not rush to nail Diana in her coffin—especially not with unctuous demands to let her "rest in peace." London's Hyde Park is now home to a controversial but undeniably permanent memorial to mark in granite her status as a treasured national figure, now very much dead. As time passes, she will join the likes of the Queen Mother, far above the reach of tabloid tittle-tattle and secure in her hard-won reputation for good works. But equally, let's not artificially overpromote her saintly qualities or radiant beauty. She would be the first to scoff at the idea that she was more virtuous than any other fallible human being . . . and she was always quick to complain about the size of her nose or the clumsiness of her feet.

Instead, we should relax and enjoy the happy memories she has left us. And we should look for lessons in her fate. Her memory will fade quickly enough when it has ceased to have relevance for our contemporary reality. Meanwhile, be wary of those who try to give that fading process a helping hand.

DIANE LOUISE JORDAN

Diane Louise Jordan is a British television presenter best known for her role in the long-running children's program *Blue Peter,* which she hosted from 1990 until 1996. She is currently hosting BBC1's religious show, *Songs of Praise.* Also noted for her charity work, Diane Louise Jordan is vice president of the National Children's Home in England.

*W*e all need to be loved—whether we admit it or not. *All* of us.

A friend of mine recalled how, when in Rwanda a few years ago, he was taken to visit a lady in the slums. She was in agony because of an AIDS-related illness and had just hours to live. He described the inadequate dirt-floor shack that was her home among unbearable squalor. And yet he said it wasn't the intense poverty or painful illness that struck him most, but rather the compassion of her friend who kept vigil. A friend who used no words, just silent tears, to express the deep feelings she had for her dying companion.

In a similar way, it wasn't words that stirred international attention, but the silent image of two people holding hands. One an HIV/AIDS sufferer and the other a "fairy-tale" princess. When Diana, Princess of Wales, held the hand of that seriously ill man back in the 1980s, many boundaries were crossed, many stigmas defeated. At that time, fear of death by AIDS had gripped the world so savagely that we were in danger of losing our humanity. Yet all it took to crush the storm of fear was a simple loving gesture.

Princess Diana was good at that. She had the courage to follow her instincts, even if it meant being countercultural. She made it her job to be kind and loving.

My first impression of the Princess was mostly disappointment. For me, Prince Charles's timid young nursery nurse girlfriend lacked character. This was at a time when a lot of my female contemporaries were unashamedly outspoken—for better or worse, we were the beneficiaries of the feminist movement. So to us, Diana's quiet reserve looked weak.

And yet, even in those early days, when she often looked awkward under the glare of attention, I found her compelling. Initially, my interest in her was purely superficial. I watched fascinated as she transformed from bland "Sloane" (the informal name given to posh people who live in or around London's wealthy Kensington area) to dynamic fashion icon. It was evident that she was *much* more than her packaging.

As a BBC television host, I've had the privilege of meeting most of the Royal Family. However, I never met Princess Diana. It wasn't until after her death that I became more closely associated with her.

Despite never having met her, when her tragic death was announced, I took it personally, like countless others. How had she been able to captivate me—a complete stranger—who initially hadn't really thought that much of her? What was it about her that compelled me on so many levels? What was, and still is, the Diana Factor?

There's much that can be said about the people's princess's unique influence—much of which has been recorded many times over—but simply put, perhaps her greatest asset is that she *connected*. She *chose* to care. She understood that we all need to feel good about ourselves—we need to know we're loved. And she chose to offer support along the way, specializing in bringing into focus those on the margins who before she shone a light on them were overlooked, ignored.

When in late 1997 I was invited by the Right Honorable Gordon Brown, Chancellor of the Exchequer, to sit on the Diana, Princess of Wales Memorial Committee, I was clueless as to why I'd been chosen. I was in the middle of a filming assignment in the United States when the call came through. Sitting on the bed in my New York hotel room, still with the receiver in my hand after agreeing to the chancellor's request, I kept asking myself, "Why me?" The rest of the committee seemed to me to be high fliers of great influence *or* closely related to her. I was neither. I didn't fit.

But, perhaps, that's the point. A lot of us think we don't fit, don't believe we're up to much. Yet the truth is we're all part of something big, and we're all capable of inspiring others to be the best that they can be. This is what Princess Diana believed. The Princess influenced and inspired many through her life, and now I had an opportunity to be part of something that ensured her influence would continue.

It was our responsibility as the Memorial Committee to sift through more than ten thousand suggestions by the British public to find an appropriate memorial to the life and work of the Princess It was unanimously felt that the memorial should have lasting impact and reflect the many facets of Diana, so we came up with four commemorative projects: the Diana Nurses, a commemorative £5 coin, projects in the Royal Parks, and the Diana, Princess of Wales Memorial Award, for young people between the ages of eleven and eighteen.

The Diana Award, as it is now known, was set up to acknowledge and support the achievements of young people throughout Britain. Each year the award is given to individuals or groups who have made an outstanding contribution to their community by improving the lives of others, especially the more vulnerable, or by enhancing the communities in which they live. The Diana Award is also given to those who've shown exemplary progress in personal development, particularly if it involves overcoming adversity.

I've been associated with the Diana Award since it was established in 1999. And now, as a trustee, I'm extremely honored to be further involved, as I believe that the award holders are a *living* part of the late Princess's legacy. They represent the kind of brave, caring, idealistic values Diana admired and championed.

Like the late Princess, this award simply shines a light on what is already there, already being achieved. It's as if Diana herself is telling the recipients how fantastic they are. The Princess said her job was to love people, and through this award she is still doing that.

Recently, I was at an award holders ceremony. I was overwhelmed to be in an environment surrounded by beautiful young people committed to wanting the best. Like Princess Diana, they all demonstrate, in their individual ways, that when we strive to do our best, whether by overcoming personal adversity or contributing to the well-being of others, it changes us for the better. We see a glimpse of how we could all be if, like Diana, we have the courage to expose our hearts.

RICHARD KAY

❧

Richard Kay became friends with Diana, Princess of Wales, through his job as royal correspondent for London's *Daily Mail*. After her separation in 1992, he used his knowledge to give a penetrating and unique insight into Diana's troubled life, and they remained friends until the end. Richard is now diary editor of the *Daily Mail* and lives in London with his wife and three children.

Six hours before Diana, Princess of Wales, was killed, she telephoned me from Paris. She told me she had decided to radically change her life. She was going to complete her obligations to her charities and to the antipersonnel-land-mine cause and then, around November, would completely withdraw from her formal public life.

She would then, she said, be able to live as she always wanted to live. Not as an icon—how she hated to be called one—but as a private person.

It was a dream sequence I'd heard from her before, but this time I knew she meant it. She wanted to finance a charity for the victims of land mines, and she had also sketched out a framework of a plan to open hospices for the dying all over the world.

And yet in the midst of all this excitement, she suddenly said, "But I sometimes wonder what's the point? Whatever I do, it's never good enough for some people."

There was a sigh and a silence. At the other end of the line was not so much a princess as a little girl who had unburdened herself and was waiting for words of comfort and understanding. She knew that whatever I said and whatever I might write, it would always be what I thought, and sometimes, necessarily, it would be critical. So she trusted me and revealed herself constantly as a person completely unrecognizable to her most vocal critics, many of whom had never met her.

Suddenly, she brightened, and we switched the subject to her boys, William and Harry.

"I'm coming home tomorrow, and the boys will be back from Scotland in the evening," she said. "I will have a few days with them before they're back at school."

She was a bit troubled that Saturday because William had called her to say that he was being required by Buckingham Palace to "perform"—they wanted him to carry out a photo call at Eton, where he was due to begin his third year the following Wednesday. What troubled Diana, and indeed William, was that the spotlight was being shone exclusively on William, who was fifteen, and not on his twelve-year-old brother, Harry.

She had told me on a previous occasion how hard it was for Harry being overshadowed by William as a second son, and she said she tried to ensure as far as possible that everything was shared—a strategy endorsed by Prince Charles.

It was on a return flight from Nepal in early 1993 that the Princess and I had our first serious lengthy conversation. It was the start of what became a friendship based on one crucial element—her complete understanding that I, as a journalist, would never sacrifice my impartiality, especially where it concerned her acrimonious differences with the Prince of Wales and certain members of the Royal Family.

Over the years, I saw her at her happiest and in her darkest moments. There were moments of confusion and despair when I believed Diana was being driven by the incredible pressures made on her almost to the point of destruction. She talked of being strengthened by events, and anyone could see how the bride of twenty had grown into a mature woman, but I never found her strong. She was as unsure of herself at her death as when I first talked to her on that airplane, and she wanted reassurance about the role she was creating for herself.

In private, she was a completely different person from the manicured clotheshorse that the public's insatiable demand for icons had created. She was natural and witty and did a wonderful impression of the Queen. This was the person, she told me, that she would have been all the time if she hadn't married into the world's most famous family.

What she hated most of all was being called "manipulative" and privately railed against those who used the word to describe her. "They don't even know me," she would say bitterly, sitting cross-legged on the floor of her apartment in Kensington Palace and pouring tea from a china pot.

It was this blindness, as she saw it, to what she really was that led her seriously to consider living in another country where she hoped she would be understood.

The idea first emerged in her mind about three years before her death. "I've got to find a place where I can have peace of mind," she said to me.

She considered France, because it was near enough to stay in close touch with William and Harry. She thought of America because she—naively, it must be said—saw it as a country so brimming over with glittery people and celebrities that she would be able to "disappear."

She also thought of South Africa, where her brother, Charles, made a home, and even Australia, because it was the farthest place she could think of from the seat of her unhappiness. But that would have separated her from her sons.

Everyone said she would go anywhere, do anything, to have her picture taken, but in my view the truth was completely different. A good day for her was one where her picture was not taken and the paparazzi photographers did not pursue her and clamber over her car.

"Why are they so obsessed with me?" she would ask me. I would try to explain, but I never felt she fully understood.

Millions of women dreamed of changing places with her, but the Princess that I knew yearned for the ordinary humdrum routine of their lives.

"They don't know how lucky they are," she would say.

On Saturday, just before she was joined by Dodi Al Fayed for their last fateful dinner at the Ritz in Paris, she told me how fed up she was being compared with Camilla.

"It's all so meaningless," she said.

She didn't say—she never said—whether she thought Charles and Camilla should marry.

Then, knowing that as a journalist I often work at weekends, she said to me, "Unplug your phone and get a good night's sleep."

The very first photograph Tim Graham took of the young Lady
Diana Spencer outside the kindergarten where she was working.

ABOVE: Diana with Prince Charles and President and Mrs. Bush outside the White House in Washington.

LEFT: Diana and her private secretary, Patrick Jephson.

ABOVE: Diana meeting actress Joan Collins for the first time at a charity benefit. BELOW: Fergie and Diana having a laugh with racegoers at Royal Ascot in the late eighties before the breakup of their respective marriages.

ABOVE: Diana and Richard Branson.

RIGHT: Diana at the Christie's party in New York to promote the sale of her dresses.

RIGHT: Diana with former MP and bestselling author Jeffrey Archer.

BELOW: Diana meets singer Liza Minnelli after the performance of her one-woman show.

Diana with land-mine victim Sandra Txijica in Angola. A picture worth a thousand words, forever linking the Princess to the campaign against the horrors of land mines.

LEFT: Diana with fashion designer Zandra Rhodes at the Christie's party in New York.

RIGHT: Diana and her trusted personal protection officer Ken Wharfe waiting to present prizes at a polo match.

BELOW: Diana with her friend designer Bruce Oldfield at a Barnardo's Ball in the mid-1980s. The Princess was president of the charity and was wearing an off-the-shoulder Oldfield frock of purple velvet.

The royal Princes Charles, William, Harry, and Philip, accompanied by Diana's brother, Earl Charles Spencer, walking behind the Princess's coffin as it enters Westminster Abbey.

LARRY KING

❧

Larry King is one of the premier figures in American broadcasting, and his show, *Larry King Live*, on CNN, is one of the longest-running television programs currently on the air. The summer of 2007 will mark his fiftieth anniversary in broadcasting.

I first met Princess Diana at a party in Los Angeles. As at so many parties in LA, there were famous people from all walks of life—actors, broadcasters, executives, authors, politicians, journalists. But there was only one princess, and she stood out from the crowd, talking and smiling and taking the time to give each person some personal attention. I kept her in the corner of my eye, waiting for an opportunity to talk to her. But she was spending so much time with every guest! Eventually, I made my way over to where she stood, and waited for a chance to finally meet this illustrious lady.

Her pictures did not do her justice. I had seen her many times on TV and in the papers, of course, but seeing her in person was a whole new experience. She was absolutely beautiful. Her face was radiant, animated and full of life. She had honesty in her eyes, which made her approachable, and she had this uncanny ability to make everyone around her comfortable. I have interviewed thousands of people in my career, and this is a quality that I've always known is essential for a broadcaster. But for Diana, it seemed to come completely naturally. Within the first five seconds of meeting her, I felt like we had been friends for years.

It was a big party and she was the star. Everybody wanted to talk to her. Not a big surprise—after all, she had interesting things to say about so many different topics. I always respected her work with land mines and AIDS, I knew her importance to the fashion world, and her role as a princess in the Royal Family made her one of the hottest topics of the tabloids. Yet she chatted about her sons and her friends with everybody—Diana was an extraordinary woman with an unassuming air, and it was an absolute pleasure to be in her presence.

When we were introduced, her eyes lit up and she grabbed my hand. She said, "Oh, you're Larry from the telly!" We laughed and spoke for a little while about our families, and I was amazed at how well she remembered all of the little details I mentioned. After all of the people she had met that night, she was bright-eyed and curious about everything. My only regret from the first time we met was that we didn't have a few more hours to talk!

I blushed when she mentioned a few interviews I had done earlier in the year. I didn't know she had seen me on CNN. It was a warm, friendly greeting that I will never forget.

TWIGGY LAWSON

British supermodel Twiggy Lawson is often regarded as one of the most important fashion icons of the modern era. Entering fashion at the age of sixteen, Twiggy revolutionized the international modeling world in the 1960s. She is also a prolific actress and activist, recently appearing as a judge on CW's *America's Next Top Model*.

About a year before that fatal day in Paris, I was invited to the opening of Richard Avedon's photographic exhibition at the National Portrait Gallery. I had not seen Richard for more than twenty years, so I was looking forward to catching up with him. Also, I was told that I would be featured in the exhibition. To me, Avedon is *the* great fashion photographer of the twentieth century, so I was thrilled to be part of the exhibition of his work.

Moreover, Princess Diana was to open the event. Having been a huge fan of hers, I was also very excited to actually be meeting her. Being a woman in the public eye, and having experienced a little of what she went through, I also felt very sorry for the constant intrusion on her life by the media.

Leigh (my husband), our son Jason, and I arrived at

the gallery before Diana arrived. We walked in and were taken over to say hello to Avedon. As we turned into the gallery, I was totally amazed, because the opening photograph (which, incidentally, was an enormous poster size) was a head shot of me taken in the late 1960s for American *Vogue*. It had always been a favorite of mine. So I was thrilled.

It was lovely to see Dick Avedon again, and we chatted away while waiting for Diana to arrive. The organizers told us she had requested that she be photographed with us under my portrait, which I thought was lovely. I was a little nervous—but I needn't have been. She arrived surrounded by her usual bodyguards and assistants, but immediately came over to Richard, Leigh, Jason, and me and started chatting. She was so lovely, natural, and funny. She asked me lots about working with Avedon, and I felt like I'd known her for years. When she was asked to walk through the exhibition, she asked us to join her, and we were thrilled to do so. I kind of felt she was holding out a hand of friendship to us, and that she felt comfortable with us. At one point, looking at a photo of a beautiful model, she asked Jason (about twenty years of age then) what he thought. He expressed his admiration of the photograph and the model, and she said that William and Harry would love it, too.

My instinct was to pull her to one side and invite her to have dinner with us at San Lorenzo (a mutually favorite restaurant in London's Knightsbridge) after the exhibition, but I knew she probably had to go on to an official dinner. I knew she would have much more fun with us, and how I wish I had done it. I wrote her a thank-you note the following day, expressing our delight in meeting her. I was amazed to get a very prompt reply expressing much the same, and saying how important her children were to her, and that she loved the fact that we were so close to ours.

I had always planned to eventually contact her and invite her to a private, casual dinner at our house, but sadly, that was never to be.

I'm so happy we met, but like the rest of the world I am so sad she was taken away too early. She was fragile and strong, like a wonderful flower.

DARREN McGRADY

Darren McGrady was personal chef to Princess Diana until her tragic accident. He is now a private chef in Dallas, Texas, and a board member of the Pink Ribbons Crusade: A Date with Diana. His cookbook, titled *Eating Royally: Recipes and Remembrances from a Palace Kitchen,* will be released in August 2007 by Rutledge Hill Press. His website is located at www.theroyalchef.com.

I knew Princess Diana for fifteen years, but it was those last four years after I became a part of her everyday life that I really got to know her.

For me, one of the benefits of being a Buckingham Palace chef was the chance to speak to "Lady Di." I had seen her in the newspapers; who hadn't? She was beautiful. The whole world was in love with her and fascinated by this "breath of fresh air" member of the Royal Family.

The first time I met her, I just stood and stared. As she chatted away with the pastry chef in the Balmoral kitchen, I thought she was even more beautiful in real life than her pictures in the daily news. Over the years, I've read account after account of how the Princess

could light up a room, how people would become mesmerized by her natural beauty, her charm, and her poise.
I couldn't agree more.

In time, I became a friendly face to the Princess and
was someone she would seek out when she headed to
the kitchens. At the beginning, she would pop in "just
for a glass of orange juice." Slowly, her visits became
more frequent and lasted longer. We would talk about
the theater, hunting, or television; she loved *Phantom of
the Opera* and played the CD in her car. After she and
Prince Charles separated, I became her private chef at
Kensington Palace, and our relationship deepened as
her trust in me grew. It was one of the Princess's key
traits; if she trusted you, then you were privy to everything on her mind. If she had been watching *Brook-
side*—a UK television soap opera—then we chatted
about that. If the Duchess of York had just called her
with some gossip about "the family," she wanted to
share that, too. "You'll never believe what Fergie has
just told me," she would announce, bursting into the
kitchen with excitement. She loved to tell jokes, even
crude ones, and would laugh at the shock on my face—
not so much because of the joke, but because it was the
Princess telling it. Her laughter was infectious.

The Princess was a pleasure to cook for. I had prepared all the wrong kinds of foods for her at Balmoral, Sandringham, and Windsor during the years when she was afflicted with bulimia. But as her private chef at Kensington, I helped her eat healthy, mostly organic meals. She loved fruit and vegetables and made a conscious effort to eat right and exercise. She began working out at the gym three days a week. Her life was back on track, and she was looking the best she had for a long time. She threw herself into public life and was a committed patron of 119 charities. That meant lots of entertaining.

When she did entertain, always for lunch, the Princess made sure to keep the guest list small so that she could speak with everyone around the table. She believed in direct conversation and an informal atmosphere.

But she didn't wait for the world to come to her. I remember once she popped into the kitchen to ask for an early lunch. "I have to go and meet a little girl today that has AIDS, Darren," she said. "Your Royal Highness"—I called her that until the day she died— "what do you say to a little girl with AIDS?" "Well, there is not a lot I can do or say," she replied, "but if just by sitting with her and chatting with her, perhaps making her laugh at my bad jokes, I can take her mind off her pain for just that short time, then my visit will have been worth it." Those words stuck with me and had an impact. After the Princess's death, I moved to America as a personal chef and got heavily involved in charity work—and she was right.

HEATHER MILLS

As a tireless campaigner for many charitable causes, Heather Mills joined Diana in support of the banishment of land mines all over the world. For her efforts against land mines, Ms. Mills was awarded the inaugural UNESCO Children in Need Award. She is also Goodwill Ambassador for the United Nations Association, and she has been active in helping amputees by promoting the use of prostheses.

*D*iana, Princess of Wales, was a truly remarkable human being. All too often today we refer to people as icons; in Diana's case, the word is wholly appropriate. She was a wife, a mother, a humanitarian, and a true ambassador.

Despite what the press wanted us to believe, Diana didn't court publicity. On the contrary, she did far more behind the scenes to help people than in front.

Her willingness to reveal her own frailties has, I am sure, encouraged many people to seek help and come to terms with their own personal problems.

She was able to reach out to people in a way that few can. In the early days of HIV and AIDS, when everyone was so afraid of this so-called new disease,

Diana's simple gesture of shaking hands with an AIDS patient at a hospital in London broke down the taboo and removed the stigma around the disease. Her palace advisers had initially tried to dissuade her from making this gesture, but Diana—who always led with her heart—went against them and did what she believed to be right.

The memory of Diana walking through a minefield is how I remember her the most. We had been campaigning for years, and struggling to get people to sign the mine-ban treaty. When Diana decided to help, a great light was shone on the cause, and we have never looked back.

Her devastating death only catapulted the cause forward; every additional country that signed up for the treaty did so, I believe, as a tribute to her tireless work and dedication to helping others.

She was brave, she was genuine, she was warm, and she really cared about people. She was the people's princess.

Remember—monuments are not erected to those who criticize, but rather to those who have been criticized.

PIERS MORGAN

Piers Morgan is a British journalist best known for his editorial work for the *Daily Mirror* from 1995 through 2004. He is also a successful author and television personality whose recent credits include a recurring role as a judge on NBC's *America's Got Talent*. A controversial member of the tabloid press during Diana's lifetime, Piers Morgan established a uniquely close relationship with the Princess during the 1990s.

*L*unch with Diana. A big day—a massive, humongous day, in fact.

I got there ten minutes early, feeling decidedly nervous. The Kensington Palace front door was opened by her beaming butler. He walked me up the stairs, chatting cheerfully about the weather and my journey, as if a tabloid editor prowling around Diana's home was a perfectly normal occurrence. He said that the "Boss" was running a bit late, joking that "she'll be furious you are here first!" and invited me to have a drink. "What does she have?" I asked. "Water, usually," he replied, "but wouldn't you rather have a nice glass of wine? She won't mind in the slightest." I readily agreed, if only to calm my racing heartbeat.

He then left me alone in the suitably regal sitting room. Diana had a perfectly normal piano covered in perfectly normal family snaps. It's just that this family was the most photographed on the planet. Lots of pictures of her boys, the young heirs, perhaps the men who will kill off, or secure, the very future of the monarchy. To us, they were just soap opera stars, semi-real figments of tabloid headlines and the occasional palace balcony wave. But here they were, her boys, in picture frames, like any other adored sons.

Just sitting in her private room was fascinating. Her magazines lay on the table, from *Vogue* to *Hello,* as well as her newspapers—the *Daily Mail* at the top of the pile, obviously, if distressingly. After I had spent ten minutes on my own, she swept in, gushing: "I'm so sorry to have kept you, Piers. I hope Paul has been looking after you all right." And then came what was surely one of the most needless requests of all time: "Would you mind awfully if William joins us for lunch? He's on an exeat from Eton, and I just thought that given you are a bit younger than most editors, it might be good for both of you to get to know each other."

"I'm sorry, but that would be terribly inconvenient," I replied sternly. Diana blushed slightly and started a stuttering "Yes, of course, I'm so sorry . . ." apology, when I burst out laughing. "Yes, ma'am, I think I can stretch to allowing the future king to join us for lunch." The absurdity of this conversation held no apparent bounds. But before he joined us, Diana wanted a little chat. "How's your circulation?" she asked. Bloody rampant, I thought, as she nestled into her sofa, radiating a surprisingly high degree of sexual allure.

"Oh very healthy, ma'am, thanks to you." She laughed, a tad insincerely. We discussed her mate Fergie. "Can't you go a bit easier on her?" Diana pleaded, with genuine concern in those extraordinarily big, expressively deep, blue eyes.

"Well, she's her own worst enemy," I replied. "Look at this morning's front pages—I mean, who the hell takes the Concorde the day after the papers reveal she's £3 million in debt?"

"I know, I know," sighed the Princess, "but she means well; she has a big heart. It's not easy for her." We debated the merits of Fergie, or even Diana herself, emigrating away from the media firestorm. "Yes, but to where? I've thought about it often, but somebody would find me wherever I went." And then I saw a flash of real sadness in her face, a desperation almost to have her anonymity back, but knowing it is gone forever. I asked what it was like "being Diana." "Oh God, let's face it, even I have had enough of Diana now— and I *am* Diana." She screeched with laughter, and I saw her chameleon side. Able to switch so easily from misery to hilarity. "It's been ridiculous recently, just one thing after another. But I can't stop the press writing about me, can I? You are hardly going to say, 'Oh, okay then, we'll leave you alone.' I would like to have a good break. I meet a lot of ordinary people, and they are always so kind to me. They shout out things like 'Eh, Di, I know what you're going through, luv,' and I laugh and think: 'If only you really knew. He's worrying about his allotment or whatever, and I've got things like the future of the monarchy on my mind.'" More screeches—she has a great laugh. A really earthy infectious cackle. Like a Sloaney Barbara Windsor.

William arrived at 1 p.m., age thirteen and a half, with braces on his teeth. Tall, shy, and clearly rather bemused to be here, he nodded, rather embarrassed, in my direction. "Hello, sir," I said, totally unsure of what to call him. "Hello," he replied, preferring not to call me anything.

Jane Atkinson made up the four. We went through to a small but very pleasant little dining room to eat. William asked Diana if she'd seen the portrait of the Queen in yesterday's papers. "Her hands looked like she'd been in the garden all day; they were all big and dirty," he laughed. Diana giggled instinctively, then stopped herself. "William, please, don't say that."

"Sorry, Mummy, but it's true: Granny did look really funny."

Granny. How odd it sounded.

"Can I have some wine, Mummy?"

"No, William! Whatever are you thinking?"

"But Mummy, I drink it all the time."

"Erm, no, you don't actually, and, well, you can't have any."

"Yes, I can," he replied with a mischievous but determined grin.

And he did. A small but interesting piece of power play to observe. William knew what he wanted, and Diana was a soft touch with her boys. Both facts seemed quite good news to me. She had water. The meal was simple but very nicely prepared: salmon mousse, chicken and vegetables, ice cream, coffee. Diana ate all of hers, quite normally. If she still suffered from any eating disorder, then she hid it very well. The conversation moved swiftly to the latest edition of "Have I Got News for You."

"Oh, Mummy, it was hilarious," laughed William. "They had a photo of Mrs. Parker Bowles and a horse's head and asked what the difference was. The answer was that there isn't any!"

Diana absolutely exploded with laughter.

We talked about which was the hottest photo to get.

"Charles and Camilla is still the really big one," I said, "followed by you and a new man, and now, of course, William with his first girlfriend."

He groaned. So did Diana. Our "big ones" are the most intimate parts of their personal lives. It was a weird moment. I am the enemy, really, but we were getting on well and sort of developing a better understanding of each other as we went along.

Lunch was turning out to be basically a series of front-page exclusive stories—none of which I was allowed to publish, although I did joke that "I would save it for my book"—a statement that caused Diana to fix me with a stare, and demand to know if I was carrying a tape recorder.

"No," I replied, truthfully. "Are you?" We both laughed, neither quite knowing what the answer really was.

The lunch was one of the most exhilarating, fascinating, and exasperating two hours of my life. I was allowed to ask Diana literally anything I liked, which surprised me, given William's presence. But he was clearly in the loop on most of her bizarre world and, in particular, the various men who came into it from time to time. The *News of the World* had, during my editorship, broken the Will Carling, Oliver Hoare, and James Hewitt scoops, so I had a special interest in those. So, unsurprisingly, did Diana. She was still raging about Julia Carling: "She's milking it for all she's worth, that woman. Honestly. I haven't seen Will since June '95. He's not the man in black you lot keep going on about. I'm not saying who that is, and you will never guess, but it's not Will."

William interjected: "I keep a photo of Julia Carling on my dartboard at Eton."

That was torture. That was three fantastic scoops in thirty seconds. Diana urged me to tell William the story of what we did to Hewitt in the *Mirror* after he spilled the beans in the ghastly Anna Pasternak book. I dutifully recounted how we hired a white horse, dressed a *Mirror* reporter in full armor, and charged Hewitt's home to confront him on allegations of treason with regard to his sleeping with the wife of a future king—an offense still punishable by death.

Diana exploded again. "It was hysterical. I have never laughed so much." She clearly had no time for Hewitt, despite her "I adored him" TV confessional. "I knew he was selling stories to the papers, and as for Anna Pasternak, she was clearly seduced by him," she said.

On the Oliver Hoare fiasco and *those* cranky phone calls, she said: "I know where it came from. It caused me a lot of damage, didn't it? People thought I was mad."

"What's been the most upsetting thing you've had to read about yourself?"

"Well, those pictures the other day of my supposed cellulite upset me a lot actually. It really hurt me. It was too painful, too personal. It's my body everyone was talking about, not just my face. I felt invaded because they put the cameras deliberately onto my legs."

Diana's relationship with the paparazzi was obviously complex. She professed to hate them: "I know most of the paparazzi and their number plates. They think I am stupid but I know where they are. I've had ten years practice. I would support an antistalking bill tomorrow."

Then she took me to the window and started showing me the various media cars, vans, and motorbikes lurking outside.

But when I asked why she doesn't go out of one of the ten other more discreet exits, she exposed her contrary side: "I want to go out the front like anyone else. Why should I change my life for them?" "Because it would make your life easier?" I said. William was equally upset by the constant prying lenses: "Why do they have to chase my mother around so much? It's unfair on her." I was torn between genuine concern for the young man protecting his mum so gallantly, and a sense of foreboding for him that one day it would be him, not his mother, who would be chased just as aggressively. How do you explain to a thirteen-year-old boy that he sells papers and therefore he's a valuable commodity to photographers and editors like me?

When Diana was photographed in full makeup actually watching a heart operation in the theater, it sparked not a little controversy. But she was unrepentant. "That little boy is alive and well and coming to see me at the palace. The charity got loads of publicity and benefited hugely, and I'd do it again tomorrow. The others were wearing makeup and jewelry; nobody told me I couldn't. I didn't even think about it."

The rest of the lunch was a random romp through her extraordinary tabloid life.

"Do you regret doing *Panorama*?"

"I have no regrets. I wanted to do it, to put my side over. There has been so much rubbish said and written that it was time people knew the truth. But I won't do it again. Once is enough. I have done what I set out to do."

I mentioned I'd been in contact with her mother.

"Oh crikey, that sounds dangerous!"

"She's a feisty woman, isn't she?"

William giggled. "Granny's great fun after a few gin and tonics."

"Sh, William," Diana said, giggling too. "My mother's

been a tremendous source of support to me. She never talks publicly; she's just there for me."

"And what about William's other granny?"

"I have enormous respect for the Queen; she has been so supportive, you know. People don't see that side of her, but I do all the time. She's an amazing person."

"Has she been good over the divorce?"

"Yes, very. I just want it over now so I can get on with my life. I'm worried about the attacks I will get afterward."

"What attacks?"

"I just worry that people will try and knock me down once I am out on my own."

This seemed unduly paranoid. People adored her.

I asked William how he was enjoying Eton.

"Oh, it's great, thanks."

"Do you think the press bother you much?"

"Not the British press, actually. Though the European media can be quite annoying. They sit on the riverbank watching me rowing with their cameras, waiting for me to fall in! There are photographers everywhere if I go out. Normally loads of Japanese tourists taking pictures. All saying 'Where's Prince William?' when I'm standing right next to them."

"How are the other boys with you?"

"Very nice. Though a boy was expelled this week for taking ecstasy and snuff. Drugs are everywhere, and I think they're stupid. I never get tempted."

"Does matron take any?" laughed Diana.

"No, Mummy, it gives her hallucinations."

"What, like imagining you're going to be king?" I said.

They both giggled again.

"Is it true you've got Pamela Anderson posters on your bedroom wall?"

"No! And not Cindy Crawford, either. They did both come to tea at the palace, though, and were very nice."

William had been photographed the previous week at a party at the Hammersmith Palais, where he was mobbed by young girls.

I asked him if he'd had fun. "Everyone in the press said I was snogging these girls, but I wasn't," he insisted.

Diana laughed. "One said you stuck your tongue down her throat, William. Did you?"

"No, I did not. Stop it, Mummy, please. It's embarrassing."

He'd gone puce. It was a very funny exchange, with a flushed William finally insisting: "I won't go to any more public parties; it was crazy. People wouldn't leave me alone."

Diana laughed again. "All the girls love a nice prince."

I turned to more serious matters.

"Do you think Charles will become king one day?"

"I think he thinks he will," replied Diana, "but I think he would be happier living in Tuscany or Provence, to be honest."

"And how are you these days—someone told me you've stopped seeing therapists?"

"I have, yes. I stopped when I realized they needed more therapy than I did. I feel stronger now, but I am under so much pressure all the time. People don't know what it's like to be in the public eye, they really don't. Look at poor Michael Barrymore."

The TV comic had recently been treated in a clinic for alcohol and drug addiction, and I'd heard rumors that Diana had been secretly comforting him.

"I feel so sorry for Michael; he is so good on TV, so funny. It would be awful if it ends for him. I hope he gets better soon. His whole family has sold him down the river, which is terrible."

We'd finished our coffee. The lunch was over. Two bizarre hours that had flashed by like some high-octane fireworks display. The Princess took me downstairs back to the real world, asking me as we walked not to tell James Whitaker, our royal correspondent, too much about our lunch. "Just throw him a morsel every six months to drive him mad," she said.

"He's a terrible skier," said William. We stepped out into the forecourt. Diana shook my hand, then darted over to speak to my very excited driver. As she shook his hand, too, she reached for his ample neck and exclaimed: "Ooh, what a nice tie—is it from Tie Rack?" It was. He will never wash it again. What a gal. I sat in the car, and started frantically scribbling notes. I didn't want to forget any of this.

BRUCE OLDFIELD, OBE

Bruce Oldfield graduated from St. Martin's School of Art in London at the age of twenty-three. He immediately staged a one-man show in New York for Henri Bendel, returning to London to show his first collection. He opened his first ready-to-wear and couture shop in 1984. His autobiography, *Rootless,* was published in 2004. He has also designed for several films and more recently refurbished a Georgian and Victorian terrace in Newcastle.

She was still Lady Diana Spencer when she first wore one of my frocks. It was November 1980, and she had chosen a navy-blue velvet divided skirt and jacket to wear to turn on the Christmas lights in London's Oxford Street. Diana used to go to the offices of *Vogue* and choose from a selection they had picked for her, so I didn't actually meet her until August 1981. It must have been after her honeymoon and she had lost a hell of a lot of weight and was quite a different shape.

My showroom was at 41 Beauchamp Place, a few doors from where I now have my shop, and I got a call from Kensington Palace to say the Princess of Wales, as she was by then, would like to come and see some designs. She arrived with her lady-in-waiting, Anne Beckwith-Smith. Although she was quite shy and seemed rather overwhelmed by the whole business of choosing clothes, she was totally charming and very kind to the staff, even bringing in flowers the next day to thank them for looking after her. It was the beginning of our friendship, and if the outfit she had chosen had been well received by the press—and in those days there were pictures of her every single day in the papers—she would ring me up and say, "We did it, didn't we!"

I realized how vulnerable she was and was very gentle and careful with her, so much so that she used to call me "oily Oldfield." But we got on extremely well. We shared a dirty sense of humor and often had lunch at San Lorenzo, a few doors away in Beauchamp Place. We gossiped and had a bit of a bitch together, but you had to be careful because she did drop people, who immediately fell so far from favor that I couldn't even mention their names. She would tell me little secrets, but nothing too personal, and I only knew when she was having problems when I sensed her mood change.

I suppose I spent the most time with her in the mid-eighties, when they called her Dynasty Di because of all the padded shoulders and glamorous frocks she wore then. The dress everyone remembers is the low-backed gold-pleated lamé dress with big shoulders that she wore for the 1985 Barnardos ball. The Princess was president of Barnardos, and I helped organize the ball because I was involved in the charity as a former Barnardos boy myself. The match of my being an orphan and her being a princess was considered a public relations dream by both the palace and the charity, so I was deemed the perfect person to accompany her.

As we walked down the stairs in the Great Room at the Grosvenor House Hotel, twelve hundred people stood up. Just at that moment, she said to me: "Bruce, I have got something for you."

I replied, "Oh God, can't it wait, ma'am?"

Then out of her handbag came a packet of Benson & Hedges—the brand of cigarettes I then smoked. Later on after the meal, she said, "Do your worst and smoke your head off," which, of course I did, much to the irritation of some of the other guests, who considered it rude before the Loyal Toast. But we had already decided there would be no Loyal Toast, and then everyone started smoking.

During the speeches, Diana kept pinching my bum to get me to move it along a bit as all she wanted was to get on the floor and dance, which we did. I remember getting onto the dance floor, which was totally empty except for me and the Princess but filled up within minutes. There was a sort of halo of people around us with a gap of about eighteen inches between us and them, so they could all look at her. She loved it. She loved being looked at. It was a star-studded occasion with people like Christopher Reeve, Charlotte Rampling, and Joan Collins, but all eyes were on Diana.

She knew she had that magnetic appeal, even in the early eighties. When people drew near to her, she turned to them with those lovely little asides—not with a stony royal response. She knew she could increase that power through her frocks and was becoming fixated on the way she was looking.

The next Barnardos ball the Princess attended was quite different. She was wearing another of my frocks—a purple velvet off-the-shoulder dress. The sample had been trimmed with mink, but she had it trimmed with ruched velvet and beading so as not to offend the anti-fur lobby. It was the dress she was photographed in that year for an official portrait. This time she was accompanied by Prince Charles. Sadly, they left early, and no one had the pleasure of watching her dance.

At the very end of the eighties, she was at the Albert Hall for another fund-raiser, and Anita, my business partner, and I flew in from Sydney, because we had been asked to take a table adjoining the royal party as a sort of "safe haven" staging post for the Princess. She and the Prince weren't getting on by then, and it showed. Diana was wearing a very sexy red bias-cut dress with a plunging back that I had made for her. It was tight across the bum so she could wiggle in it, which she liked. There is a famous picture of her and Prince Charles standing together but looking in opposite directions, which went worldwide as an illustration of how their marriage was in trouble. She looked gorgeous, but her mood was not happy.

As I provided her with many of her most regal function dresses, I began to wonder if they were a record of her bad public moments with Prince Charles. This might actually have been true, because after she gave up public duties in 1993, she never used me again.

I did not mind. My partner, the late Anita Carroll, and I had enjoyed our time with the Princess, and she helped us tremendously. One year she wore one of my dresses to the Designer of the Year awards and sat next to Ira Neimark, the president of Bergdorf Goodman. As Diana was chatting to her, she looked over at me and gave me a wink, and the next day Bergdorf Goodman placed a big order.

We shared some laughs. We shared some good times. We shared an interest in charitable causes. She was a real person. A modern princess.

ROBERT POWELL

Robert Powell is an accomplished British actor with a forty-year career that has included a bit of everything, from *Doomwatch* via *Jesus of Nazareth* and *The Detectives* to *Holby City* on television, from *Mahler* via *Tommy* to *The Thirty-Nine Steps* in films, and from *Hamlet* via the Royal Shakespeare Company to Alan Bennett's *Single Spies* in the theater. And the highlights? Three for twelve at Lord's and a hole in one at Sunningdale!

In 1989, I was making a series called *Hannay* for Thames Television when the boss of Thames, Sir Ian Trethowan, asked me if I would chair a celebrity committee that he was putting together to support the charity Help the Aged.

That is how I found myself sitting opposite the Princess of Wales, the patron of Help the Aged, at the charity's annual awards ceremony at London's Hilton Hotel. It was at the height of her stardom, and although there were plenty of rumors that all was not well in her marriage, none of us knew that anything was amiss. She was charming, charismatic, and very chatty. I don't think the conversation ever got round to the charity we were both there to represent, as we talked almost exclusively about television—what her favorite programs were and what the young princes enjoyed. I remember she was delightfully uncritical, taking care never to mention anything she didn't like, unlike anyone else with whom I've ever had a conversation on the subject!

The impression of the Princess that I gained over that lunch was that she didn't have a deeply intellectual attitude about anything. She was interested in the very few things other than television that we did discuss, but her opinions seemed to be instinctive rather than considered. This didn't make her any less enchanting, but I did come away feeling that the union with Prince Charles was possibly not a perfect match. Prince Charles is very passionate about a number of issues, but his interests tend to be intellectual, as opposed to Diana's deeply emotional concerns.

Oddly enough, I thought Diana photographed better than she actually looked. She was very pretty, but I confess that I was not as smitten as most men seemed to have been when in her company. Aside from that, it was easy to see how she could use her immense charm to devastating effect. And I confess to being extremely flattered when on another occasion she spotted me in the crowd and waved a "Yoo-hoo" at me!

Afterward, I remembered that I had narrated the

video documentary of Charles and Diana's 1981 wedding that was put out by ITN. It was probably just as well that I didn't mention it over lunch, as I doubt whether it would have been a happy subject for conversation.

In retrospect, what is curious about the Princess's unhappiness is that she can't have been that much taken by surprise when she joined the Royal Family. Albeit a child of a broken marriage, she was the daughter of an earl who had himself been around royal circles for a good deal of his life as a former equerry to King George VI and had lived on the Sandringham estate. In other words, I think she may have had an inkling of what she was in for. If that was the case, then the popular vision of Diana as victim does look a little less realistic. I suspect that naively Diana had ambitions of her own, and that one of them was to be a happy princess.

Like everyone else, I was saddened by Diana's death. But it was a tragedy, not a catastrophe. From the moment the event was hijacked on the Sunday morning by Tony Blair's "people's princess" speech (which, incidentally, I turned off after thirty seconds, I was so appalled) to the deeply unfortunate speech made by her brother at the funeral, what should have been a time for personal grieving turned into a maelstrom of hysteria.

Under any other circumstances, the Royal Family's initial decision to stay at Balmoral, where the two boys could be quietly and gently cared for, would seem to be sensible. I believe the family must have been desperately hurt by the reaction of the "people's tabloids." They don't reflect bigotry; they create it.

ALBERTO REPOSSI

Since opening his first shop in the Hotel Hermitage in Monte Carlo in 1977, Alberto Repossi has remained one of the most distinguished and sought after jewelry designers in the world. He was commissioned in the mid-nineties to design a ring for Diana and Dodi Al Fayed, and he continues to design for many notable royal families and cultural figures.

Against my will did I have the unhappy privilege of being related, together with our house, to a terrible tragedy that sprang from a love story.

H.R.H. Princess Diana was attracted by the modernity and sobriety of my creations, and I was overwhelmed by such an important recognition, since for me the Princess perfectly embodied the image of the modern woman.

When I was told about the crash, I realized it was my duty and that of our house to defend discretion at any cost, and thereby the memory of H.R.H. Princess Diana.

I first tried to do so in pleading professional ethics, then in showing evidence to whoever wanted to discredit such a person.

I hope that now, after ten years, the time has come when conjectures have died off and everyone remembers her elegance and follows her legacy of kindness and charity.

As for me, as a designer, I shall have in mind an image that shall always be a source of inspiration.

I only have one regret: a meeting that will never take place.

ZANDRA RHODES

Zandra Rhodes is a British fashion designer who specializes in innovative textile design. Internationally recognized for her glamorous and dramatic style, she was honored by Queen Elizabeth II in 1997 and made a Commander of the British Empire. Currently in high demand by the rich and famous worldwide, Zandra designed many garments for Diana during the nineties.

Princess Diana married very young. She was a perfect, unspoiled flower with a strong, generous inner spirit, which she was probably unaware of when she married Prince Charles. She was thrust unprepared into the position of future queen of England. She had to grow up and mature in front of the public eye. That public eye was hard, judgmental, and unforgiving. Her strong inner spirit guided her to do things that normally someone in her position would not do—it would have been suppressed. Diana acted in a very genuine, caring, and natural way.

I was bicycling to work in London along the leafy Bayswater Road in very casual working clothes when a huge official limousine passed me. Against the rear window were two beautiful hats; the car was obviously going to Ascot. The two young girls in the car were waving at me (very enthusiastically), one with golden corn-colored hair and the other one blond. They looked exactly like Princess Diana and Sarah Ferguson, the Duchess of York. I thought, "It cannot be them, they would not be so friendly, casual, and outgoing, and anyway, it's the wrong side of Kensington Palace, and cars going to Ascot do not come along this road." I pretended I had not seen them and carried on cycling.

A few weeks later, I was fitting the Princess in Kensington Palace and she said to me, "Are you still riding your bike?" "Yes," I replied. It was not until I left and drove my car out of the palace grounds that I realized the route took me exactly to the Bayswater Road, where I had seen the two waving girls!

Princess Diana always tried to make me feel at home when I was fitting her. She would talk about the problems of being recognized: how she came out of her gym in Kensington High Street in the pouring rain and bumped into a famous actor. As he entered the street, he hunched his shoulders and put on dark glasses. Princess Diana said to him, "I hope they disguise you more than they do me!"

SIR CLIFF RICHARD

With more than 150 singles, albums, and EPs to reach the top twenty in the United Kingdom, British pop star Sir Cliff Richard is one of the most successful musicians in the UK's recent history. Knighted by Queen Elizabeth II in 1995, Sir Cliff Richard was the first rock star ever to receive the national honor.

I wonder whether Prince William and Prince Harry will remember their first Royal Command Performance? I was skiing at Lech, in Austria, and Princess Diana and the boys were staying at the same hotel. Somehow Princess Diana got to hear of the sing-alongs my party had in the hotel bar as part of the après-ski, and she asked me whether I'd mind singing for her sons one evening.

Well, it was as close to a royal command as you could get, so there I was, rattling off all my old 1960s hits, and there were William and Harry trying hard to stifle yawns! It was Harry who suddenly chirped up in the most regal of voices, "I say, do you know 'Great Balls of Fire'?" I did, and that night Diana and the boys heard probably the most energetic rendition ever!

I can't say I got to know Diana well, but I did meet

her on a number of social, as well as formal, occasions, and she was always so charming and so gracious. At a dinner at the home of a mutual friend, she was the first to volunteer to don the rubber gloves and tackle the washing up.

I was in New York at the U.S. Open tennis tournament in September 1997, not thinking for a moment that I'd be invited to her funeral. When I received a call from my secretary to say an invitation had arrived, I booked the next Concorde flight home for another, this time incredibly tragic, royal command.

RAKESH ROSHAN

Rakesh Roshan is a producer, director, and actor in Bollywood films. A member of the successful Roshan film family, Mr. Roshan opened his own production company in 1982 and has been producing Hindi movies ever since. His film *Kaho Naa . . . Pyaar Hai* won nine Filmfare awards, including those for best movie and best director.

I didn't have the privilege of meeting Diana personally, but as a keen observer I learned a lot about her through the media and television coverage of her various activities and her visits to various countries, including India. I vividly remember when she came to my country and visited places that interested her, such as Mother Teresa's Missionaries of Charity, various homes of the destitute, orphanages, hospitals, and so on. On all of these occasions, her kind looks, kind words, and kind actions, such as holding the poor orphan children in her lap, caring for them with love, and wiping their tears, were sufficient indications to convey the passion that Diana had in her heart for the service of the poor and underprivileged. Wherever she went, she went with such noble mission. She derived a sort of divine pleasure through her visits to charitable institutions, orphanages, and homes of the destitute. By minutely looking at her, one could see a deity in Diana—dedicated to love and kindness—devoted to charity and goodness and the darling of all she met. For such human virtues, love for the poor and concern for the suffering of humanity, Diana commands the immense respect, admiration, and affection of the whole world. Wherever she went, she was received with genuine affection and warmth, unlike politically staged receptions.

When I remember Diana and her activities in the last years of her life, I strongly feel that God sends some special people into this world to perform some special duties. Diana was one of these special people. Advancing on this godly path of love and goodness, Diana was blossoming like a flower, and with her captivating fragrance she started infusing new life in our dangerously sick garden—which was apparently at the brink of a precipice. The irony is that the cruel winds of autumn ruthlessly blew away this rare flower and deprived the world of its soothing fragrance. Diana, Princess of Wales, is no longer present in this world, but Diana, the queen of millions of hearts, is immortal and will live forever.

My heart breaks when I think of her last journey, her funeral, which was brilliantly covered all over the world. One could see the whole of England in tears, and the eyes of all the television viewers were also flooded. Thousands of men, women, and children had lined up along the entire route from the palace to the church where the services were held. All the fresh flowers available in the United Kingdom were there on the passage. All eyes were tearful, and one could clearly hear the sobs of people. There were heartrending scenes of people paying tribute to their departed darling.

Last, I would like to write here a translation in English of a poem written in Urdu.

We hope you will come back . . . dear friend
But why this pervading sadness . . . dear friend
The familiar flavor in the atmosphere is singing . . .
You are somewhere around . . . dear friend

Please come back, Diana; this sinking world desperately needs a savior.

DAVID SASSOON

For several decades, British designer David Sassoon has provided the best in evening wear for fashionable and famous customers from his high-profile store in London. His work has been featured in many international fashion shows and museums throughout the world, and his garments are in high demand at such notable stores as Saks Fifth Avenue, Harrods, and Neiman Marcus.

The Princess of Wales would often make surprise visits to my shop, as I had made her going-away dress and many other outfits for her trousseau.

In August 1982, Diana came to my shop with Lady Sarah Armstrong-Jones, the daughter of Princess Margaret, who had been a bridesmaid at Diana's wedding.

The Princess was wearing a blue-and-white-striped sailor-style two-piece outfit; Sarah wore a white shirt and a cotton skirt, as it was a very hot day.

Diana said that she would like to choose a long evening dress for Sarah as a present. The dress was to be worn at a ball at Balmoral Castle. This was Sarah's first long dress, and Diana wanted her to have her dream dress.

There were lots of giggles and excitement as Diana helped Sarah try on some of the dresses, and the dressing room was full of laughter.

Finally, Sarah chose a bright red strapless taffeta ball dress, which made her feel very grown up.

We brought them tea while the dress was being fitted, and Sarah, who obviously adored Diana, listened to her advice about what accessories would complement the dress.

Sarah was so excited about her beautiful and glamorous present when they left the shop. Diana had made a young girl's dream come true.

INGRID SEWARD

Ingrid Seward is editor in chief of *Majesty* magazine and has been writing about the Royal Family for more than twenty years. She is acknowledged as one of the leading experts in the field and has written ten books on the subject. Her latest book, *Diana: The Last Word,* with Simone Simmons, will be published in paperback in 2007 by St. Martin's Press.

A few weeks before Diana's tragic death in the summer of 1997, I received a telephone call from her private secretary to say the Princess wanted to see me. She explained that the Princess was both amused and irritated by an article I had written in London's *Daily Mail* and felt it was time we got together. I can't remember exactly what I had written, but the gist of it was that guests were secretly coming into Diana's Kensington Palace apartment hidden under a rug in the back of a car and entering through a door that could not be seen by security cameras. It could, however, be seen from Princess Margaret's apartment opposite, which was how I came by the information.

The invitation was typical of Diana, as she instinctively knew there was no better way of getting her message across than to confront her antagonists and make them her friends. What I didn't know at the time was that Diana was terrified that I had discovered her secret affair with Hasnat Kahn, the Pakistani doctor with whom she was in love and who used to come into her apartment hidden under a rug in her butler's car. I had in fact no idea who she was hiding, as at that time, no one knew she was romantically involved with Hasnat Kahn.

It was 11 a.m. on one of those hot humid days of her last summer when I arrived at apartments 8 and 9 in Kensington Palace, where the Princess lived. The front door was open so I walked straight in. It took a few minutes before I found her butler, Paul Burrell, who apologized for not greeting me, and showed me to the loo. The walls were hung with cartoons depicting various events in Diana's life (including one of a huge pile of horse dung, which said, "Has anyone seen James Hewitt?"). Paul Burrell then led me upstairs to the main sitting room—or salon, as it was called—on the first floor and disappeared to make some coffee.

Minutes later, Diana breezed into the room. Despite the relatively early hour, she was dressed as if she was about to leave for a cocktail party. She wore an electric-blue sleeveless dress—a Versace, she told me. Her shoes were Chanel, her jewelry understated but expensive.

Diamond and sapphire earrings with a thin, diamond-studded Cartier "line" bracelet on one wrist, a gold watch on the other. When she moved, a faint whiff of scent stirred in the morning air. She assured me in her breathy, little-girl voice that she was not annoyed with me; she just wanted to have a "girlie chat."

We talked about everything and everybody, jumping from one subject to another as only women can. She was wonderfully indiscreet, and I found myself asking her the kind of things that I would hardly dare ask a close friend. I had recently been to the Ritz Hotel in Paris as Mohamed Al Fayed's guest with Diana's stepmother, Raine Spencer. At one time Diana hated Raine, but she had revised her opinion, and they were now the greatest of friends. As Raine worked for Harrods, the subject of Mohamed came up. Diana confessed she found him very amusing and "naughty," and we joked that even the soap in the bathrooms of the Ritz Hotel was probably bugged. Diana was far more astute than people gave her credit for, and she knew a lot about Mohamed. He had invited her to see the Windsor House in Paris and bring William and Harry, and although she had wanted to go she had refused, saying, "Didn't dare put my head over the parapet on that one."

In retrospect, it makes it all the more strange that only a couple of weeks later she accepted an invitation to spend a holiday with the Al Fayed family. But I guess she changed her mind, or simply decided she didn't care what the "family"—meaning the Royal Family—thought anymore.

We also talked about the Duchess of Windsor. Diana told me that the Queen had paid all the duchess's medical bills in her last years, and when she was buried at Frogmore, Diana, who was there with Prince Charles, saw the Queen cry for the first and only time in her life.

Of course, our conversation got round to the subject of men. Diana hoped that one day she might be able to find a man who could "cope" with her (this was before her romance with Dodi Al Fayed). She told me of her love for Prince Charles and explained that despite all the public rows and disagreements, they had reached an understanding based on the deep affection they still held for each other. She hated the public perception that she had entered into a loveless marriage and wanted to put the record straight.

"Charles did love me," she said. "It's very upsetting for the boys to hear that their father did not love me. If anyone could see the letters he wrote me at the beginning or have seen us on the day of the separation, they would have known that. We both sat on the sofa and cried."

My daughter, who was eight at the time, was born on the same day in the same hospital delivered by the same doctor as Harry (several years later, of course), and this gave us a mutual bond and an excuse to bring up the subject of the two princes. Diana explained that William was a typically sensitive Gemini, while Harry was livelier and could cope with anything. She then went on to tell me how much she wanted another child, and she told me Harry was always asking her to have another baby so he didn't have to be the youngest. She had to explain to him it might be better if she got married first!

Although Diana assured me that she was happy and finally felt she had found a real purpose in her life, I could still sense some of her inner turmoil. When we were gossiping, she was relaxed, but when we moved on to more serious matters, such as her treatment by the media, her body language betrayed her anxiety. She wrung her hands and looked at me out of the corner of her startling blue eyes. "No one understands what it is like to be me," she said. "Not my friends, not anyone."

She admitted, however, that there was a positive side to her unique situation in that she could use her high profile to bring attention to the causes she cared about, and this, she assured me, was what she was doing now and wanted to do in the future. But it was the darker, negative side that she had to live with every day. After all this time, she explained, it still upset her to read untruths about herself, and it was simply not in her nature to ignore it.

"It makes me feel insecure, and it is difficult going out and meeting people when I imagine what they might have read about me that morning."

Diana had no idea how much she was loved. To the poor, the sick, the weak, and the vulnerable, she was a touchstone of hope. But her appeal extended much further than that. She had the ability to engage the affections of the young and the old from all walks of life.

That summer, she wrote a birthday letter to my daughter that read, "I hope for your birthday you man aged to get those grown-ups to give you a dolls' house and the cardigan and the pony hair brush you wanted. Don't believe their excuses."

She wrote similar letters to thousands of other people and always in her own hand. The effect was magical. "Please don't say anything unkind about her. She's my friend," our daughter instructed her father.

That, I think, explains the extraordinary outpouring of grief we witnessed when Diana died. Her appeal was as simple as it was unique. Diana touched the child in each and every one of us.

She wasn't the "people's princess"—she was the people's friend.

The words of a London cabbie still ring in my ears when I think about the week after her death.

"We'll never see the like of her again," he said as he dropped me off near the ocean of flowers outside Buckingham Palace.

He was right.

NED SHERRIN

Ned Sherrin is a satirist, novelist, anthologist, film producer, and celebrated theater director who has been at the heart of British broadcasting and the arts for more than fifty years.

I had met Diana, Princess of Wales—perhaps "I had been presented to" is more accurate—in lineups after charity shows that I had been compering and at which she was the royal guest of honor. There were the usual polite exchanges.

On royal visits backstage, Princess Alexandra was the most relaxed, on occasion wickedly suggesting that she caught a glimpse of romantic chemistry between two performers and setting off giggles. Princess Margaret was the most artistically acute, the Queen the most conscientious; although she did once sweep past me to get to Bill Haley, of whom she was a fan. Prince Edward could, at one time, be persuaded to do an irreverent impression of his older brother, Prince Charles. Princess Diana seemed to enjoy herself, but she was still new to the job and did not linger down the line.

Around this time, a friend of mine opened a restaurant in London. From one conversation, I gathered that although it was packed in the evenings, business was slow at lunchtime. Soon afterward, I got a very "cloak-and-dagger" phone call from him. He spoke in hushed tones, muttering something like "Lunch next Wednesday, small party, royal person, hush-hush."

From this, I inferred that he wanted me and, I had no doubt, other friends to bring a small party to dress the restaurant, to which he was bringing the "royal person" in a bid to up its fashionable appeal during the day.

When Wednesday dawned, the luncheon clashed with a couple of meetings, and although feeling disloyal, I did not see how I was going to be able to round up three or four people—even for a free lunch. Guiltily, I rang his office and apologized profusely to his secretary for not being able to make it.

The next morning, he telephoned, puzzled and aggrieved.

"There were only going to be the four of us," he said. "Princess Diana had been looking forward to meeting you properly. She was very disappointed that you couldn't make it."

I felt suitably stupid—but, as luck had it, a few weeks later I found myself sitting next to her at a charity dinner at the Garrick Club. I explained the whole disastrous misunderstanding, and we had a very jolly time laughing at the coincidence that she was dining at this exclusive club before her husband, who had just been elected a member with some publicity. Prince Charles was in the hospital at the time recuperating from a polo injury. Although hindsight tells us that the marriage was already in difficulties, that was not generally known, so in answer to my inquiries, she replied sympathetically that he was recovering well.

We talked a lot about the theater and her faux pas some years before when she had been to Noel Coward's *Hay Fever* and confessed to the star, Penelope Keith, that it was the first Coward play that she had seen.

"The first," said Penelope, shocked. "Well," Diana said to me, "I was only eighteen!"

Our meeting was at the height of the AIDS crisis, and as we were both working a lot for AIDS charities, we had many notes to compare and friends to mourn. The evening ended with a dance—but being no Travolta myself, I doubt that my partnering was the high point for her.

SIMONE SIMMONS

Simone Simmons works as an energy healer, helping her patients through empowering them rather than creating a dependency on the healer. She specializes in absent healing, mainly with sufferers of cancer and AIDS. She met Diana four years before her death when the Princess came to her for healing, and they became close friends. In 2005, Simone wrote a book titled *Diana: The Last Word*.

*D*iana was exuberant about everything she did, and that extended to her friendships. She didn't so much walk into a room as explode, scattering smiles and jokes and good humor in a way that embraced everyone. When she saw someone she knew, her face would light up, her arms would fly out in welcome, and more often than not she would wrap them in a warm hug, while new acquaintances were made to feel like old friends.

Very few are blessed with that kind of star quality, and we were all captivated by her charisma. It was almost as if she was skipping on air, and even those who had been critical of her in the past came away enchanted after spending only a short time with her.

Whenever we met, she always made me feel as if she was truly grateful for my time and exuded interest in everything I was doing. Most of us try and hide our insecurities behind a mask. Diana never bothered with that sort of psychological subterfuge. She was refreshingly open and interested in everyone around her in an unaffected and outgoing way that shone through in her photographs, which I am sure is why she enjoyed such enormous popularity.

No person can operate in a vacuum, of course, and Diana needed support and encouragement from her confidantes. She was surrounded by people, but there were not many she could really talk to. She had a lot of acquaintances, but few real friends: too few. With friendship comes a certain amount of intimacy, of sharing your feelings and innermost thoughts, and there were not many people she could confide in. Because she was the Princess of Wales, many people were too dazzled by her status to see the whole person.

Try as she might, she could not switch the princess role on and off like a light switch. Marriage to Prince Charles had removed her from ordinary life in a way she had not foreseen, and it was a long struggle to rediscover the simple pleasures of giving and sharing confidences.

The most important thing I did with Diana over

the four years I knew her well, when we met almost every day and spent hours on the telephone, was to teach her how to heal. This enabled her to bring real comfort to the many hundreds and thousands of seriously ill people she met. Nothing was too lowly or demanding for her to tackle. She embraced people suffering from leprosy and AIDS. She cuddled the wounded and the sick. Diana was so committed to her work that she learned to channel her remarkable gift as a healer to aid the afflicted.

It was while I was teaching her to meditate that I started to train her to channel her energies toward those she was in contact with. She picked this up very quickly, and once she got the knack of it, she used to practice on her sons, William and Harry, her friends, and the people she met through her charity work. She was a tactile person and told me that when she was a child, she would always snuggle up to whoever was reading her a bedtime story, as she liked the feeling of human contact. On her visits to hospices and hospitals, she would hold the people's hands and look directly into their eyes so they could feel her love and energy flowing forth. She explained, "Nothing gives me greater joy than trying to help the most vulnerable members of society. It's my one real goal in life—a destiny."

I realized Diana had been born with an extraordinary ability, which had only been waiting to be released. By 1996, when she was fully in control of her life for the first time, she was able to give a great deal of consolation and encouragement to so many people. She received scant attention for this at the time. Everyone seemed to concentrate on the negative aspects. Instead of seeing how genuinely caring she was, they accused her of doing it for the publicity. That was utterly untrue. I often joined her when she returned from a day's work, and she would be so exhausted, she found relief in crying. She was anxious about what she had seen and experienced and was determined to find something she could do to help.

Her late-night visits to hospitals were supposed to be private. She knew how frustrating it is to be alone in a hospital; the staff and patients were always very surprised and pleased to see her. She used to make light of it and say, "I just came round to see if anyone else couldn't sleep!" Although Diana saw the benefits of the formal visits she also made, and she did get excited when money poured in for her charities, she much preferred these unofficial occasions. They allowed her to talk to people and find out more about their illness and how they were feeling about themselves, in a down-to-earth way without a horde of people noting her every word. She wasn't trying to fill a void or to make herself feel better. To her, it was not a therapy to help other people: It was a commitment born of selflessness.

Diana was forever on the lookout for new projects that might benefit from her involvement. Her attention was caught by child abuse and forced prostitution in Asia. We had both seen a television program showing how little children were being kidnapped and then forced to sell themselves for sex. Diana told me she wanted to do everything she could to eradicate this wicked exploitation taking place in India, Pakistan, and most prevalently in Thailand. As it turned out, it was one of her final wishes. She didn't have any idea of exactly how she was going to do it, and hadn't got as far as formulating a plan, but she would have found a way. When Diana put her mind to something, nothing was allowed to stand in her way. As she said, "Because I've been given the gift to shine a light into the dark corners of this world, and get the media to follow me there, I have to use it," and use it she did—to draw attention to a problem and in a very practical way to apply her incredible healing gifts to the victims. In her fight against land mines, she did exactly that.

If anyone ever doubted her heartfelt concern for the welfare of others, this cause must surely have dispelled it. It needed someone of her fame and celebrity to bring the matter to the world's attention, and her work required an immense amount of personal bravery. She faced physical peril and endured public ridicule, but Diana would have seen the campaign to get land mines banned as her greatest legacy.

Helping others was her calling in life—right to the very end.

CORNELIO SOMMARUGA

As president of the International Committee of the Red Cross for more than twelve years beginning in the late 1980s, Swiss/Italian-born Cornelio Sommaruga was responsible for leading the Red Cross through many of the most difficult and troublesome conflicts in recent history. His humanitarian efforts in virtually every continent are extensive, and he was instrumental in arranging Diana's anti-land-mine campaign.

Princess Diana had visited the headquarters of the International Committee of the Red Cross at the beginning of the nineties. I had received her officially as the then president of the ICRC. We had a good dialogue, and I invited her to a simple luncheon in the ICRC building.

It must have been 1992 when I received a phone call from the British Red Cross telling me that the Princess of Wales wanted to see me. We agreed that I would fly to London for a private dinner in a hotel. We were— I think—five around the table. The interest Princess Diana had in humanitarian action was great. She asked a number of precise questions. She wanted to be active in one way or another for the Red Cross in the world.

It was at that dinner that I talked to her of my intention to launch a worldwide appeal for a total ban of antipersonnel mines. She was impressed by the description of the suffering of so many civilian victims, of their medical care and social reinsertion. She concluded the evening by saying that she would be pleased to participate in a field mission in a country mostly affected by land mines.

The British Red Cross did the follow-up. It took a couple of years. The mission of the Princess of Wales to Angola was eventually co-organized by the BRC and the ICRC. It was a tremendous success. World public opinion was made aware of the worldwide tragedy of land mines.

The Princess of Wales died—in the tragic circumstances that we know—just at the eve of the opening of the Oslo Diplomatic Conference in mid September 1997, where the Mine Ban Treaty was drafted and initialed. It was subsequently signed in Ottawa on December 2, 1997.

All those engaged in this effort will never forget the great contribution given by the Princess of Wales to the fight against land mines.

TAKI

As a prolific author and journalist, Taki has written for many top-rated publications, including the *Spectator*, the London *Sunday Times*, *Vanity Fair*, *National Review*, and many others. Greek-born and American-educated, Taki is a well-known international personality and a respected social critic all over the world.

inding something original to say about Diana is like trying to be humorous about race in a PC world. That is, it's almost impossible. She may have been the queen of hearts, but she was also a very willful woman. I was fully aware that I was being used by her throughout our four-year friendship, and enjoyed every minute of it. Let's take it from the top.

In June of 1987, I was an usher at the wedding of Harry Somerset, Marquis of Worcester, to Tracy Ward. The wedding and ensuing ball took place in the grand Ward country house, attended by a large portion of British society, including the Prince and Princess of Wales. Late in the evening, while I was in my cups, a friend, Nicky Haslam, grabbed my arm and introduced me to Diana, who was coming off the dance floor. We exchanged pleasantries, me slurring my words to the extent that she suddenly took my hand, looked at me straight in the face, and articulated, "T-a-k-e y-o-u-r t-i-m-e." She mistook my drunken state for a severe speech impediment and went into her queen-of-hearts routine. Nicky, of course, ruined it all by pulling her away and saying, "Oh, let him be, ma'am; he's drunk as usual."

We occasionally met after that and always had a laugh about it. But we never got further than that rather pathetic incident. In 1994, I began writing the "Atticus" column for the Sunday *Times,* the bestselling Sunday broadsheet in Britain. By this time Diana and Charles had separated, and Diana had gone on the offensive against what was perceived by her to be Buckingham Palace plotting. As a confirmed monarchist, I warned in one of my columns that her popularity was enough to one day bring down the monarchy. I also wrote that she was bonkers. One month or so later, at a ball given in London by Sir James Goldsmith and his daughter Jemima Khan, a mutual friend approached me and told me that Princess Diana would like to speak with me. As luck would have it, yet again I was under the weather. When I reached her table, she pulled out a seat for me and asked me to sit down. The trouble was that I missed the chair and ended up under the table. Diana screamed with laughter, pulled up the tablecloth, looked underneath, and asked me point-blank: "Do you really think I'm mad?" For once I had the right answer. "All I know is I'm mad about you." It was the start of a beautiful friendship, as Bogie said in *Casablanca*.

Diana was not as "thick as two planks" (as she described herself), but she was certainly no great thinker. She was street-smart, which was surprising for someone of her background. She had limited knowledge of history, and as far as I could tell no interest in it at all. Great ideas were for others to discuss. She liked light gossip about people she knew. She never once criticized any member of the Royal Family, at least not in my presence. What she wanted from me was access to top editors. I gave couple of dinners in my house for her and invited various Fleet Street hotshots. When she first suggested it, I demurred. Paparazzi were always one step behind, and the last thing I wanted was to have my house patrolled twenty-four hours a day by those scummy types. "Not to worry," said Diana. "I have a foolproof system."

This involved having a nondescript car somewhere in London, leaving Kensington Palace in the boot of her official car, then, after being dropped off where the other car was parked, having the chauffeur drive back to KP. "Another night alone at home" was the way she put it with a mischievous grin. Although not a close friend, I was most likely among the last people to speak with her on that fateful evening of August 31, 1997. I was in my chalet in Gstaad, Switzerland, and had Nigel Dempster, the numero uno gossip columnist of Britain, staying with me. We discussed the so-called romance between Dodi Al Fayed and Diana. I insisted then, and still do today, that it was just a publicity stunt. There was no hanky-panky between the two. Al Fayed and his father loved publicity, and Diana loved rubbing it in on the royals who had mistreated her. So I rang Diana in front of Dempster around eight in the evening. She had given me a special mobile number. She greeted me with "Hello, stranger." (I had not spoken to her for quite a while.) "This is a professional call," I told her. "Will you be wearing a chador any time soon?" She laughed. "You must be kidding," she said. "You know very well what this is all about." Three or four hours later she was dead. She died for a blurred photograph, as far as I'm concerned, and the grotesque myths and accusations that have emerged from publicity-seeking persons since her death are as disgraceful as her hounding by the paparazzi.

CHRIS TARRANT, OBE

British radio broadcaster and television presenter Chris Tarrant is perhaps best known for his role as host on *Who Wants to Be a Millionaire?* A hugely successful entertainment personality, Chris Tarrant is also active in many charitable causes, including homelessness and disadvantaged children. He was honored with an OBE in 2004 for his extensive work in these areas.

The first time I met her I was terribly nervous. I was working on the breakfast show at Capital Radio in London in those days, and I'd been seated next to her at a charity lunch. She'd become the patron of Capital's charity for needy children in London, and her appearance at our big lunch of the year made it a guaranteed sellout.

She was already probably the most famous person in the world, and I was terrified about what on earth I was going to say to her. I needn't have worried—she immediately put me at ease with an incredibly rude joke about Kermit the Frog.

Because she was our patron, we saw a lot of her over the next few years. She was great fun, and brilliant with the kids. She used to listen to my show in the mornings while she was swimming or in the gym, and she'd often say things like "Who on earth was that loopy woman that you had on the phone this morning?"

There was a restaurant in Kensington that had a series of alcoves where she'd often go to hide, perhaps with just a detective for company. I remember chatting to her one lunchtime while I was waiting for my boss to join me at my table, and she disappeared round the corner. "Hello, Richard," I said, when he turned up. "I've just been chatting with Lady Di." "Yes, of course you have," said Richard. "And there goes a flying pig!" When she reappeared a few moments later and just said, "Good-bye," on her way out, this big, tough, hard-nosed media executive was absolutely incapable of speech.

We all loved her. She was fun, a lovely, warm, long-legged girl, and it was only in later years, as she became more and more depressed and desperate at her lonely life in the cold family that she'd married into, that she became more and more withdrawn.

The night she died, I was flying in to London overnight from Toronto. At about two in the morning, half awake, I was idly flicking through a *Society* magazine, which had Charles and Diana on the front cover. "Oh my God!" said the stewardess, "They must be desperately wishing they hadn't used that picture after what's happened!" "What ever are you talking about?" I asked the woman. "Haven't you heard?" she said to me. "The news has just come through to the captain that she's been killed!" Like everyone else who first heard it, I just couldn't take it in. I nodded off for a while, and when I woke up as we landed at Heathrow, it just seemed like maybe I'd had a bad dream. It was only as I walked into the airport and saw everybody was crying that I realized that the captain's message had been accurate.

The next week on the radio, every morning was one I'll never forget. Although it was usually a very manic, upbeat show, for this one week the mood was altogether different. One of grieving, one of tragedy. The radio show that week became a kind of therapy for all sorts of people mourning on the phone lines. Hard-bitten lorry drivers and cabbies came on the line, crying their eyes out. Certain records suddenly took on a whole new tragic significance. R.E.M.'s "Everybody Hurts" and Michael Jackson's "Gone Too Soon" were asked for relentlessly. And then, of course, at the weekend we had to broadcast live coverage of the funeral.

Every street in London, apart from the route taken by the coffin to Westminster Abbey, was completely deserted. Nobody stirred—it was like the City of London had been hit by a nuclear attack. And the funeral itself was, of course, the stuff of high drama. The extraordinary speech, berating the Royal Family for how they'd treated his sister, by Charles Spencer, and Elton John somehow getting his way through "Candle in the Wind," with his voice cracking with emotion, and tears pouring down his cheeks.

Even today there has never been a satisfactory explanation for her death. There are all sorts of conspiracy theories, and so many loose ends, that perhaps we'll never know how and why this beautiful young woman died. But if you talk to any taxi driver in Paris, to this day, they will all tell you that whatever happened that night in that tunnel, it was never an accident.

PENNY THORNTON

꧁

Penny Thornton is an expert astrologer and has taught and contributed to many institutions and publications in the United Kingdom. For many years, Ms. Thornton acted as a spiritual adviser to Diana. She is the author of *With Love from Diana*, published in 1995, in which she describes their friendship during the tumultuous years in Diana's life.

Kensington Palace, London. A sunny fall day. Turning leaves and fading roses; departing swallows and busy squirrels. Flowers everywhere. Banks of them carpeting the lawns, bunches of them stacked against the railings. There are candles, too, and silver balloons, sparkling as they catch the sun. Strangers thread their way along the maze of little paths, exchanging glances, silent and wistful. There is a lump in my throat, an ache in my heart. And Diana is not at home. There is only the Diana of memory.

Rewind eleven years.

Kensington Palace, London. A sunny spring day. Almond blossoms and daffodils; wood pigeons and bumblebees. I walk up the gravel drive, my heels digging trenches as I go. I have on my favorite frock, olive-green needlecord with scarlet pockets and cuffs; in my hand, my small son's music case, bulging with charts and notes. My heart is in my mouth; my stomach is fluttering like a moth. Ahead of me is a large front door, and standing holding it open is a young man in formal dress. I have only a moment to take him in because he is suddenly eclipsed by a tall, smiling gazelle bounding out to meet me. It is Diana. The Princess of Wales.

I have my instructions. I must curtsy and say that I am pleased to meet Her Royal Highness. But as soon as I bend my knee, she giggles and insists I stop all that nonsense and please call her Diana. She is wearing a beige pencil skirt and a cream cashmere sweater. There are pearls in her ears. She is far more beautiful in real life. I am mesmerized by her sapphire eyes, faintly intoxicated by the scent of tuberose. We walk up the stairs, making small talk—the weather, the traffic, the children—and I try to come back to myself. After all, I'm there for a reason.

Some ten days before, out of the blue, I had received a call from the Princess, asking me to cast her horoscope. At first I declined, due to a pressing deadline, but on hearing she despaired of "ever seeing a light at the end of the tunnel," I agreed to see her immediately. In 1986, as far as the rest of the world was concerned, the family Wales was deliriously happy, but now it seemed my worst fears were realized. The astrology between Diana and Charles had given every indication that theirs was not to be a marriage made in heaven, and I had written extensively about the difficulties and the potential for divorce redolent in their charts.

Which is why I found myself that April day in a small sitting room seated on a pink sofa next to Diana, a witness to a painful tale emerging in fits and starts. I sensed that she was anxious about our meeting, although she disguised it artfully, telling me an amusing story, accompanied by extravagant hand gestures and arpeggios of laughter, about her helicopter trip earlier in the day. But within a matter of minutes, she was all concentration and earnestness, a little frown drawing her features together, her eyes peering intently at the glyphs and circles on the charts set out before her. I explained the many themes and patterns in the horoscope, which, in turn, inspired memories and understandings. She saw irony in many of her experiences, past and present, rolling her eyes at the admission of a minor transgression, and admitting her failings with candor and honesty. Her sense of isolation both in the marriage and within the Royal Family was palpable, and at times I reached across to her, handing her a tissue and supplying reassurance. And in this way we spent the afternoon journeying through all four seasons of emotions—she the pilot, me the navigator.

Although we were to meet and talk many other times, this is the memory I return to most often. It was an emotionally charged occasion, and the images I retain are therefore sharper and more resonant. When I think about Diana, I see her next to me on the sofa, one moment shoulders hunched, eyes downcast, a tear tracing the line of her cheek; at another, pressed back against the cushions wryly recording a recent affront. I hear her voice, its sighing cadences—her dilemmas, fears, and hopes tumbling out with the unchecked force of a dam that has suddenly burst. In my mind's eye, the room is strangely dark, the only focus of light coming from two table lamps; and, perhaps, because of the distortion that time creates I see the scene as La Tour might have painted it, all reds, golds, and amber.

It is always easier to talk to a stranger, and that afternoon I was that stranger, the first person outside Diana's innermost circle to know the full extent of her misery. Only when she talked of William and Harry did her face truly light up—in fact, from time to time, we could hear them running up and down on the floor above us. At some point, she must have pressed a bell concealed under the table, because as we were drawing to the end of our meeting, the door was thrust open and the boys rushed in ahead of the tea tray. Diana and I had been together for four hours. Day had indeed turned into night: it had been a long journey. And I had a headache. Diana, sensing something was wrong, disappeared into the room beyond, returning with two painkillers and a small jewelry box. "Open it now," she urged. Inside was a little gold box, and, sitting on the lid, perfectly crafted, was a bumblebee.

With tea over, and the boys dispatched upstairs, it was time for me to go. The afternoon had been something of a catharsis for Diana; she had come to realize that she was not as powerless as she had believed, and the situation was not as hopeless as she had feared. She understood that by helping others with their pain and despair, she could in turn heal her own. No longer was she a passive victim, but an active protagonist. She had a mission. And while at the beginning of our meeting, she had come across as a sweet and fragile person, by the end of the afternoon, a steely toughness was evident. Nonetheless, as we said our good-byes I felt I was leaving behind a prisoner. The walls of Kensington Palace may be hung with tapestries, but to Diana they were no less a prison, and once the euphoria of the day had dissipated, she would be left to find her way forward, alone. Still, I knew she had enormous courage and that the next time I saw her fulfilling some duty, whether it were planting a tree or attending a glittering function, she would be radiant, dazzling all with her beauty and humor and giving no hint of sadness.

But Diana in public is not the memory I keep; it is the private Diana—the Diana of that April afternoon. And, in a way, although I miss her, she lives in my memory quite happily; she remains eternally young, forever exquisite, her spirit inextinguishable.

DONALD TRUMP

Internationally known for his real-estate developments, Donald Trump owns many important skyscrapers in New York City as well as several casinos in Atlantic City. He has also become a widely recognized television personality, notably as executive producer and star of NBC's *The Apprentice*. He has advocated many charitable causes throughout his career, most recently hosting events for Hurricane Katrina relief.

Princess Diana had the special quality of being radiantly personable. There was no way you could diminish that aspect of her being, and I think it distinguished her from many other celebrities. When I met her, I remember being impressed with her inner and outer radiance to the extent that I associate the word with her name to this day. She was a joyful person, and that's one reason she was much admired and much loved and is still missed.

CATHERINE WALKER

Catherine Walker, a London-based French couturier, is generally credited with creating the image of Diana, Princess of Wales, through a procession of literally hundreds of beautiful garments spanning sixteen years. Walker currently dresses the new younger members of the English Royal Family as well as a host of celebrities. The designer is hardly ever interviewed and prefers to work away from the spotlight.

As a fashion designer, my pleasure in dressing clients is not about their background, height, coloring, or any of those things. It is to do with the way they hold themselves: their graceful poise if they are in tune with their bodies, and their elegance if they are at ease with themselves. My relationship with Diana, Princess of Wales, started in 1981, a few months after she was married, and it lasted sixteen years, until her death. It was a privilege to learn my craft with someone who had this grace and poise. She was a gift.

KEN WHARFE

In 1987, Ken Wharfe was appointed a personal protection officer to Diana. In charge of the Princess's around-the-clock security at home and abroad, in public and in private, Ken Wharfe became a close friend and loyal confidant who shared her most private moments. After Diana's death, Inspector Wharfe was honored by Her Majesty Queen Elizabeth II at Buckingham Palace and made a Member of the Victorian Order, a personal gift of the sovereign for his loyal service to her family. His book, *Diana: Closely Guarded Secret,* is a *Sunday Times* and *New York Times* bestseller. He is a regular contributor with the BBC, ITN, Sky News, NBC, CBS, and CNN, participating in numerous outside broadcasts and documentaries for BBC—Newsnight, Channel 4 News, Channel 5 News, News 24, and GMTV.

*M*y memory of Diana is not her at an official function, dazzling with her looks and clothes and the warmth of her manner, or even of her offering comfort among the sick, the poor, and the dispossessed. What I remember best is a young woman taking a walk in a beautiful place, unrecognized, carefree, and happy.

Diana increasingly craved privacy, a chance "to be normal," to have the opportunity to do what, in her words, "ordinary people" do every day of their lives—go shopping, see friends, go on holiday, and so on—away from the formality and rituals of royal life. As someone responsible for her security, yet understanding her frustration, I was sympathetic. So when in the spring of the year in which she would finally be separated from her husband, Prince Charles, she yet again raised the suggestion of being able to take a walk by herself, I agreed that such a simple idea could be realized.

Much of my childhood had been spent on the Isle of Purbeck in Dorset, a county in southern England approximately 120 miles from London; I remembered the wonderful sandy beaches of Studland Bay, on the approach to Poole Harbour.

The idea of walking alone on miles of almost deserted sandy beach was something Diana had not even dared dream about. At this time she was receiving full twenty-four-hour protection, and it was at my discretion how many officers should be assigned to her protection. "How will you manage it, Ken? What about the backup?" she asked. I explained that this venture would require us to trust each other, and she looked at me for a moment and nodded her agreement.

And so, early one morning less than a week later,

we left Kensington Palace and drove to the Sandbanks ferry at Poole in an ordinary saloon car. As we gazed at the coastline from the shabby viewing deck of the vintage chain ferry, Diana's excitement was obvious, yet not one of the other passengers recognized her. But then, no one would have expected the most photographed woman in the world to be aboard the Studland chain ferry on a sunny spring morning in May.

As the ferry docked after its short journey, we climbed back into the car and then, once the ramp had been lowered, drove off in a line of cars and service trucks heading for Studland and Swanage. Diana was driving, and I asked her to stop in a sand-covered area about half a mile from the ferry landing point. We left the car and walked a short distance across a wooded bridge that spanned a reed bed to the deserted beach of Shell Bay. Her simple pleasure at being somewhere with no one, apart from me, knowing her whereabouts was touching to see.

Diana looked out toward the Isle of Wight, anxious by now to set off on her walk to the Old Harry Rocks at the western extremity of Studland Bay. I gave her a personal two-way radio and a sketch map of the shoreline she could expect to see, indicating a landmark near some beach huts at the far end of the bay, a tavern or pub, called the Bankes Arms, where I would meet her.

She set off at once, a tall figure clad in a pair of blue denim jeans, a dark-blue suede jacket, and a soft scarf wrapped loosely around her face to protect her from the chilling, easterly spring wind. I stood and watched as she slowly dwindled in the distance, her head held high, alone apart from busy oyster catchers that followed her along the water's edge.

It was a strange sensation watching her walking away by herself, with no bodyguards following at a discreet distance. What were my responsibilities here? I kept thinking. Yet I knew this area well, and not once did I feel uneasy. I had made this decision—not one of my colleagues knew. Senior officers at Scotland Yard would most certainly have boycotted the idea had I been foolish enough to give them advance notice of what the Princess and I were up to.

Before Diana disappeared from sight, I called her on the radio. Her voice was bright and lively, and I knew instinctively that she was happy, and safe. I walked back to the car and drove slowly along the only road that runs adjacent to the bay, with heath land and then the sea to my left and the waters of Poole Harbour running up toward Wareham, a small market town, to my right. Within a matter of minutes, I was turning into the car park of the the Bankes Arms, a fine old pub that overlooks the bay. I left the car and strolled down to the beach, where I sat on an old wall in the bright sunshine. The beach huts were locked, and there was no sign of life. To my right I could see the Old Harry Rocks—three tall pinnacles of chalk standing in the sea, all that remains, at the landward end, of a ridge that once ran due east to the Isle of Wight. Like the Princess, I, too, just wanted to carry on walking.

Suddenly, my radio crackled into life: "Ken, it's me—can you hear me?" I fumbled in the large pockets of my old jacket, grabbed the radio, and said, "Yes. How is it going?"

"Ken, this is amazing, I can't believe it," she said, sounding truly happy. Genuinely pleased for her, I hesitated before replying, but before I could speak she called again, this time with that characteristic mischievous giggle in her voice. "You never told me about the nudist colony!" she yelled, and laughed raucously over the radio. I laughed, too—although what I actually thought was "Uh-oh!" But judging from her remarks, whatever she had seen had made her laugh.

At this point, I decided to walk toward her, after a few minutes seeing her distinctive figure walking along the water's edge toward me. Two dogs had joined her and she was throwing sticks into the sea for them to retrieve; there were no crowd barriers, no servants, no police, apart from me, and no overattentive officials.

Not a single person had recognized her. For once, everything for the Princess was "normal." During the seven years I had worked for her, this was an extraordinary moment, one I shall never forget.

Diana:

A TIME LINE

IMPORTANT MOMENTS IN
THE LIFE OF THE PRINCESS

JULY 1, 1961
Diana Frances Spencer is born near Sandringham, Norfolk, on the east coast of southern England. The youngest daughter of the late Earl Spencer and the late Honorable Mrs. Shand Kydd, Diana joined two older sisters, Jane and Sarah, and would be followed by a brother, Charles.

SEPTEMBER 1970
Diana is sent to her first boarding school, Riddlesworth, in Norfolk. Although she is not the best student, she excels at ballet and sports, specifically diving and swimming.

NOVEMBER 1977

After graduating from West Heath secondary school in Kent in July, Diana encounters Princes Charles at a party at the Spencer estate in Northamptonshire.

SEPTEMBER 1980

Diana and Charles are first spotted as a couple by British journalists in Balmoral. Their relationship sparked in July during a weekend of polo, during which they both stayed with mutual friends Commander Robert and Philippa de Pass.

FEBRUARY 24, 1981

The engagement between Diana and Charles is announced to the world. Diana is only nineteen years old; Charles is thirty-two.

JULY 29, 1981

Diana and Charles are married at St. Paul's Cathedral in London, one of the most watched events in recent history. Hundreds of thousands of onlookers line the streets to see the couple married, while an estimated 750 million people tune in on television. Diana wears a lace wedding dress made of ivory silk taffeta with a twenty-five-foot train.

JUNE 21, 1982

Diana gives birth to their first child, Prince William Arthur Philip Louis. Prince William is second in line to the throne after Charles.

MARCH–JULY 1983

Diana and Charles tour the world, including a six-week visit to Australia and New Zealand. They end in Canada with a three-week visit to Ottawa and Edmonton.

SEPTEMBER 15, 1984

Diana gives birth to their second child, Prince Henry Charles Albert David, who is promptly nicknamed Harry.

APRIL 1987

During a time when many were still ignorant about HIV and AIDS, Diana makes the important gesture of shaking hands with a man suffering from the disease during the opening of the United Kingdom's first specialized AIDS ward. Her warmth toward AIDS patients helped considerably in dispelling the fear of those afflicted throughout the world.

JUNE 1991

Prince William suffers serious injuries in a golfing accident. He is struck in the side of the head by a golf club, causing a skull fracture. Diana stays with William in his hospital room throughout the recovery process.

MARCH 1992

Diana's father, Earl Spencer, dies of a heart attack.

JUNE 1992

Following a period of public speculation about the state of the royal marriage, the controversial book *Diana: Her True Story* is released. In the book, Andrew Morton reinforces this speculation by detailing the troubled reality of the relationship between Diana and Charles.

AUGUST 1992

The tabloid press continues to report heavily on Diana's personal life. The *Sun* prints transcripts of phone conversations between Diana and James Hewitt, her riding instructor, who affectionately calls her "Squidgy."

DECEMBER 1992

Prime Minister John Major announces the separation of Diana and Charles. At this point, however, there are no public plans for a divorce.

DECEMBER 1993
Diana begins drawing away from the public sphere.

MAY 1994
Diana and a Finnish student save a drowning man from a pond in London's Regent's Park.

JUNE 1994
Prince Charles confesses to adultery on the television documentary *Charles: The Private Man, The Public Role.*

NOVEMBER 1995
Diana admits to her affair with James Hewitt in a major television interview. In regard to Charles's affair with Camilla Parker Bowles, Diana comments, "There were three of us in this marriage."

DECEMBER 1995
Queen Elizabeth II sends a letter to Charles urging him and Diana to divorce. He concurs, and in a few months Diana and Charles agree to seek a divorce.

AUGUST 1996
Diana and Charles make their divorce official and agree on joint custody of the children. Diana receives a sizable settlement, and is allowed to keep her title of

"Princess." However, she may no longer be called "Your Royal Highness."

JANUARY 1997
Diana launches her major campaign against land mines in Angola, riling government officials with her call for a sweeping, international ban.

JUNE 1997
Christie's auction house sells off seventy-nine of Diana's gowns in New York City. The auction raises $4.5 million, which Diana immediately gives to worldwide AIDS and cancer research charities.

JULY 1997
Photographs surface of Diana with her new boyfriend, Dodi Al Fayed, on the French Riviera.

AUGUST 1997
Diana arrives in Bosnia to continue her campaign against land mines. She returns to Dodi soon after her trip is over.

AUGUST 31, 1997
While speeding away from paparazzi, the vehicle in which Diana, Dodi, and chauffeur Henri Paul are riding

crashes in a tunnel in Paris. They are killed in the accident. Trevor Rees-Jones, Diana's bodyguard, survives the crash.

SEPTEMBER 2, 1997
Many thousands travel to London to pay tribute to Diana, leaving a sea of flowers in front of Kensington Palace.

SEPTEMBER 4, 1997
Amid the tremendous public reaction to Diana's tragic death, Queen Elizabeth II participates in the mourning. She announces that the British flag will fly at half-mast at Buckingham Palace in honor of Diana.

SEPTEMBER 6, 1997
Diana's funeral is held at Westminster Abbey in London. Hundreds of thousands of people line the streets in London, while many millions in more than sixty countries watch on television as her body leaves Westminster Abbey and is carried to her final resting place. Diana is buried on an island on the Althorp estate.